A Clinician's Guide to Neurodivergence

I0092190

A Clinician's Guide to Neurodivergence: Supporting a Neuro-Affirmative Form of Practice is a concise handbook which provides a comprehensive and accessible overview of a range of conditions to support clinicians working with individuals with diverse neurocognitive profiles. It provides a practical guide for clinicians to move towards a more neuro-aware and neuro-affirmative way of working. It sets out guidance around diagnosis and access to services whilst giving consideration to the adaptations and accommodations that might be necessary to avoid the inequities that can often be experienced through neuro-normative or heteronormative practices.

Topics covered include learning difficulties such as dyslexia and dyscalculia, autism, ADHD, acquired brain injury and various other neurodivergent profiles. The intersection of neurodivergence with factors such as gender and age and comorbidity with mental health and personality profiles is also considered. Drawing on the NICE guidelines, the International Classification of Disease (ICD) system, and the Diagnostical Statistical Manual (DSM), each chapter provides the background to different neuro-cognitive profiles, common indicators that may be observed, screening and diagnostic assessment, clinical recommendations and signposting to relevant resources and services.

The handbook is valuable reading for students, researchers, clinicians, therapists, medical and allied professionals who require an introductory text providing in-depth details regarding a range of neurodivergent conditions.

Sarah Ashworth-Watts is a Consultant Forensic Psychologist working clinically within neuropsychological rehabilitation and independently completing risk and diagnostic assessments for individuals within the criminal justice system, as well as giving evidence at court as an expert witness. As a founding member of ABC Psychology, she has a particular interest in neurodiversity within forensic contexts, ensuring psychological provision is accessible to all. She enjoys contributing to the professional development of the next generation of psychologists, peers, and other professionals. As an Honorary Assistant Professor, she lectures and examines at academic institutions, provides specialist training worldwide, and authors multiple articles, chapters and books.

Natalie Brotherton is a Consultant Clinical Psychologist with extensive experience working with adults with a broad range of neurocognitive profiles. Her focus is adapting approaches to best meet the needs of neurodivergent people, with a particular interest in understanding and working therapeutically with people who have co-occurring forensic, mental health or personality needs. She provides training nationally and is a visiting lecturer at a European university. She is a founding member of ABC Psychology.

Hannah Carton is a Forensic Psychologist currently working with adults in a secure setting. She has worked with service users with a wide range of presentations and is committed to ensuring equity of access to service provisions. She constantly strives to develop her clinical practice skills and broader knowledge. She takes pride in providing a safe supervisory space for trainee psychologists enabling them to contribute to the development of their field of study. As a founding member of ABC Psychology, and an autistic, dyslexic practitioner herself, she has a vested interest in expanding knowledge, understanding and acceptance for neurodivergent people.

A Clinician's Guide to Neurodivergence

Supporting a Neuro-Affirmative Form of Practice

Edited by
Sarah Ashworth-Watts, Natalie Brotherton and Hannah Carton

Routledge
Taylor & Francis Group

LONDON AND NEW YORK

Designed cover image: Getty Images

First published 2026
by Routledge
4 Park Square, Milton Park, Abingdon, Oxon OX14 4RN

and by Routledge
605 Third Avenue, New York, NY 10158

Routledge is an imprint of the Taylor & Francis Group, an informa business

British Library Cataloguing-in-Publication Data
A catalogue record for this book is available from the British Library

ISBN: 978-1-032-83980-6 (hbk)
ISBN: 978-1-032-83978-3 (pbk)
ISBN: 978-1-003-51065-9 (ebk)

DOI: 10.4324/9781003510659

Typeset in Times New Roman
by Taylor & Francis Books

Contents

Illustrations

Figures

Tables

Contributors

Emma Woodhouse, Neurodevelopmental Specialist Emma has worked in clinical and research settings for the past 20 years, specialising in autism and ADHD. She feels passionately about supporting individuals and families across the lifespan and has a particular interest in working with autism within the criminal justice system. She is co-director of Compass Psychology and provides autism diagnostic assessment training for professionals across the UK and internationally.

Dr Melanie Hobbs, Psychiatrist Mel has worked in a wide range of specialties within mental health since graduating from Leicester Medical School in 2009. She gained her Certificate of Completion of Training in General Adult Psychiatry in 2019 and moved into Neuropsychiatry in 2021. Over her career she has worked with many people with autism and attention deficit hyperactivity disorder. Through this experience she has come to realise that an understanding of neurodiversity is essential for any health professional, whatever area of physical or mental healthcare they work in. She is keen to help others develop their knowledge and skills in this area to make sure all neurodiverse people receive the standard of care they are entitled to.

Kayleigh Wain, Speech and Language Therapist Kayleigh is a Speech and Language Therapist with a wide breadth of experience in various clinical specialisms such as acquired brain injury, neurological rehabilitation, learning disability and autism. She is an independent therapist and has a special interest in maximising individual capacity and autonomy within mental capacity law. Alongside clinical work, she is reading Law with a view to combine her communication skills with a future career in the justice sector. She is devoted to supporting people to find their voices and advocates strongly for quality and excellence in patient care.

Dr Lyn Shelton, Consultant Forensic Psychologist Lyn Shelton is a Consultant Forensic Psychologist with a history of working in prisons and secure services where she specialised in working with clients with learning disabilities, autism, and sexual and violent offenders. She currently works for a private health company, having clinical oversight of mental health services including early intervention for children and young people, intensive personalised support and autism assessment; she has a passion for early identification to ensure the correct support and intervention is put in place. She has published articles, amongst others, in the field of learning disability and well as authoring book chapters.

Dr Jessica Newcombe, Special Educational Needs Assistant Headteacher For over 15 years Jessica has worked in the specialist education sector in the East Midlands. She is currently Assistant Headteacher in a special school and has worked in both the primary and secondary phases. She holds a doctorate in special education. She enjoys discovering evidence-based practice and using and applying well-researched theoretical approaches to benefit children and young people. In her spare time, she enjoys spending time with her four boys, and when she has a chance, she enjoys swimming, running and walking.

Ruth Farrar, Occupational Therapist Ruth has been practising Occupational Therapy for over 20 years. She has worked predominately in mental health settings, including forensic, acute mental health and CAMHS, and works in both the NHS and privately. She has worked across the lifespan with a range of conditions and has a particular interest in neurodiversity. She uses Sensory Integration in her practice daily and is passionate about supporting individuals to recognise how sensory processing challenges can impact on their daily life. Ruth is an Advanced Sensory Integration Practitioner and within her NHS role is developing and raising the profile of how Sensory Integration as part of occupational therapy can support people to live a life worth living. She mentors students on their path to achieving their Sensory Integration Practitioner status, nationally and internationally.

Preface

Alongside professional experience and training, the editors of and contributors to this book have experience of neurodivergence either by having partners, family or friends who are neurodivergent or through being neurodivergent themselves. This has provided it with a unique set of challenges and opportunities in the process of editing this manuscript, and we believe that this has added to the value of the final version. Furthermore, each chapter's author brings with them their own specialist knowledge, professional experience and personal viewpoints on the topics discussed. We have attempted to edit the content throughout for consistency; however, this variety is reflective of the field in general and one of the many reasons we believe this area is so diverse and ever evolving.

That being said, before you set about reading this book, we would like to convey to the reader our stance and our humility in respect of our knowledge and experience of neurodivergence. To adapt a phrase coined by Thomas Lynch, the founder of Radically Open Dialectical Behaviour Therapy, we propose that 'if we know anything about neurodivergence, it is that we don't know everything and neither does anyone else'.[1] We recognise that everyone's neurology and experience is different and that the available knowledge and language around neurodivergence changes quickly. This means that some of the language we use within the book may already be considered outdated (e.g. the deficit language used in diagnostic criteria) and more still is likely to become outdated during and after publication. Similar can be said of the diagnostic manuals referenced within this book; at present the choice to use the DMS-5-TR or the ICD-11 is stipulated by services or decided upon by the individual clinical practitioner based on preference and professional judgment. However, the 2025 update of the Assessment, Formulation, and Diagnosis Guidelines for Adults[2] (BPS, 2025), which is currently out for consultation, specifies the exclusive use of the ICD-11[3] in the UK.

The aim of the handbook is to provide an introduction to any clinician starting their journey in learning about working with neurodivergent people. Whilst there is ever-increasing literature in this field, this often appears to lean more heavily towards autism and therefore we wanted to bring together an accessible introduction that included several different neuro-cognitive profiles that include those that are developmental in nature and those acquired during the lifespan. Our aim was to describe some of the common characteristics that might represent different profiles, the assessment methods and tools that might be used in identifying these, and to highlight some of the co-occurring difficulties that individuals may experience. Finally, we set out some of the reasonable adjustments/accommodations that clinicians might consider employing to assist in making the environment more accessible, and fair, to those people with whom they have the privilege to work.

Notes

1 Thomas Lynch's original phrase being 'If I know anything, it is that I don't know everything and neither does anyone else' (Lynch , M. P. 2004. Truth and Multiple Realizability. *Australasian Journal of Philosophy*, 82(3): 384–408. DOI: 10.1080/713659875).
2 A national framework to deliver improved outcomes in all-age autism assessment pathways: guidance for integrated care boards.
3 The ICD-11 is the only diagnostic manual which applies to the NHS in England. The DSM-5-TR is the official diagnostic manual used across the United States; it does not have official status in the NHS in England. Despite this, given its global prominence, criteria within the DSM-5-TR are often referred to in clinical guidelines, discussions, and reports.

1 Introduction

Emma Woodhouse

NEURODEVELOPMENTAL SPECIALIST

Whilst psychology may not have emerged as a separate discipline until the late 1800s, its roots can be traced back to ancient civilisations. For thousands of years, philosophers and physiologists have contemplated the reasons for human behaviours and debated the roles and significance of different bodily organs. In 335 BC, Aristotle understood the role of the brain as a radiator to prevent the heart (considered the most important organ at this time) from overheating. By the 1600s, Descartes theorised that the mind and body were two distinct entities that interact to form the human experience [1]. Fast forward to the 1800s and we see the development of the Diagnostic and Statistical Manual of Mental Disorders (DSM) and the International Classification of Diseases (ICD). These diagnostic systems, in their various iterations, have attempted to conceptualise 'conditions' and 'disorders' by identifying clinical characteristics which cluster together in a particular way and lead to "significant impairment" in functioning.

Of course, the ways in which psychiatric and neurodevelopmental conditions have been conceptualised, described and understood have changed considerably across different versions of the DSM and ICD. Some conditions have been removed from the diagnostic systems completely and others are now described in ways that are very different from their original conceptualisation. Diagnostic exclusions and the parameters around diagnostic criteria have also changed.

Scientific and technological advancements throughout the 20th century saw the introduction of neuroimaging and genome sequencing, enhancing our understanding of psychiatric and neurodevelopmental conditions. Research into underlying genetic and environmental factors, the interplay between these and their potential role in psychiatric and neurodevelopmental conditions is ongoing. As research continues and our understanding develops, the categorisation of difference and the landscape of assessment and diagnosis will continue to evolve.

DOI: 10.4324/9781003510659-1

The DSM and ICD are grounded in the medical model and have received criticism for many reasons. One key criticism is that these diagnostic systems focus on deficits, and that these deficits are defined by neuronormative Western values and assumptions. The 1990s saw the emergence of the neurodiversity movement, which challenged the pathologisation of neurological and neuropsychological difference. As the neurodiversity movement has gained momentum, there has been a shift away from deficit-based descriptors which underpin the medical model. There is growing recognition of the many strengths associated with neurodivergence and the importance of moving towards a neuroinclusive society.

As Dr Nick Walker summarises,

> A lot of people hear *neuro* and they think, *brain*. But the prefix *neuro* doesn't mean *brain*, it means *nerve*. The *neuro* in *neurodiversity* is most usefully understood as a convenient shorthand for the functionality of the whole bodymind and the way the nervous system weaves together cognition and embodiment. So, *neurodiversity* refers to the diversity among minds, or among bodyminds.
>
> [2]

Neuropsychology focuses on ways in which cognitions and behaviours are related to the brain and the rest of the nervous system. Each and every one of us has a unique neuropsychological profile, which inevitably comes with strengths and vulnerabilities. Some of these strengths and vulnerabilities may remain relatively stable across the lifespan, others may change over time and/or fluctuate depending on context. Whilst there is no question that there are strengths in difference, it is important to recognise that some individuals with particular neuropsychological profiles and characteristics may require specific support.

When it comes to vulnerabilities and difficulties associated with particular neuropsychological characteristics, individuals may experience and describe these in different ways. Some people may experience persistent impairment as a direct result of a neuropsychological characteristic or set of characteristics. Others may have a more dynamic experience and/or find that in the right environment and/or with appropriate support, the impairment reduces or even ceases to exist at all. Due to the unique experiences of each individual, it is important that assessment of support needs is person-centred, individualised and collaborative.

Although there are criticisms of the medical model, it is a dominant approach in the UK and diagnostic assessment is a key part of this. To be referred for a diagnostic assessment, there is usually identification of qualitative differences that appear to be causing some kind of functional impairment. If these qualitative differences are missed (perhaps due to more subtle or non-stereotypical presentations of certain characteristics, diagnostic overshadowing, compensatory strategies and/or sociocultural biases) then support needs may go unrecognised and unmet. It is important for professionals to understand the heterogeneity within different conditions in order to recognise the potential need for a referral and subsequent support.

In the absence of clear diagnostic biomarkers, clinicians are reliant on obtaining detailed information with the help of clinical assessment tools to make diagnostic decisions. The diagnostic process may include initial screening assessments, followed by more detailed interviews and observational and/or cognitive assessments. Clinicians must use information from multiple sources and consider differential diagnoses when making judgments about whether particular diagnostic criteria are met. The diagnostic process also requires clinicians to consider what constitutes expected variation within the general population vs. clinically significant characteristics in the context of a formal diagnosis.

Any attempts to fit complex, overlapping characteristics into specific diagnostic categories will inevitably be fraught with complications. Whilst some individuals may clearly meet a particular set of diagnostic criteria outlined in the DSM and/or ICD, this is not always the case. Very often, neuropsychological profiles do not fit neatly into specific categories, and as Lorna Wing highlighted, *'nature never draws a line without smudging it"* [3]. Research also indicates high rates of co-occurrence between different neurodevelopmental conditions and mental health conditions [4] which can add further layers of complexity to diagnostic assessment processes.

In addition to complexities around co-occurring and overlapping clinical characteristics, intersectionality is a crucial consideration for all clinicians and services. Whilst a person's neuropsychological profile can be very significant, life may also be shaped by intersecting factors and identities such as gender, sexuality, race and socio-economic background [5]. Understanding intersectionality and the impact of compounded forms of discrimination is essential if we are to move towards a truly neuroinclusive society. This requires us to recognise and address inherent biases within multiple systems, including everything from academia, research, professional bodies, clinical tools and processes, all the way through to service accessibility and support provision.

Whatever your stance on the medical model, diagnostic labels and use of terminology, it is important to recognise that some people require specific support in relation to aspects of their neuropsychological profile. A diagnostic label may be incredibly beneficial for some, but this alone does not automatically provide information about how to support an individual. Whilst there may be some core principles that are helpful to consider (for example, aspects of the sensory environment and preferred methods of communication), there is heterogeneity within any diagnostic category. The purpose of a comprehensive assessment is not to simply rule a diagnostic label in or out – it should provide a nuanced insight into the individual's unique profile of strengths and support needs, which can be used to develop meaningful recommendations collaboratively.

Support needs may be the direct result of a particular neuropsychological characteristic or set of characteristics, a mismatch between their neuropsychological profile and their environment, or a combination of both. It is important to recognise that many people experience barriers due to environments and systems being structured according to neuronormative values and assumptions. Neuroinclusivity requires adaptations across all societal systems at micro and macro levels. Whilst there have been improvements in recent years, there is still a lot to be done as we work towards a more neuroinclusive society.

As professionals, our development of knowledge and skills is an ongoing process. The variation and complexity of neuropsychological profiles mean that even after many years of experience, there are always ways to deepen our understanding and enhance our ways of working. This book has been written by highly experienced clinicians, with the aim of helping professionals to develop their understanding and skills when working with particular neurodevelopmental conditions and neuropsychological profiles. Each chapter focuses on a specific area, providing background information, exploring variation in presentations and highlighting important considerations for professionals. Each chapter also provides information about screening and specialist assessments, as well as adaptions and signposting. Case studies have been developed from clinical experience and are used to illustrate the application of research theory to clinical practice.

References

1. Mehta, N. (2011). Mind-body dualism: A critique from a health perspective. *Mens sana monographs*, 9(1), 202. doi:10.4103/0973-1229.77436.
2. Walker, N. & Raymaker, D. M. (2021). Toward a neuroqueer future: An interview with Nick Walker. *Autism in adulthood*, 3(1), 5–10. doi:10.1089/aut.2020.29014.njw.

3. Wing, L. (2005). Reflections on opening Pandora's box. *Journal of autism and developmental disorders*, 35(2), 197–203. doi:10.1007/s10803-004-1998-2.
4. Gotham, K., Cassidy, S. & Weiss, J. (2020). Mental health across the lifespan. *Autism*, 24(4), 805–808. doi:10.1177/1362361320912132.
5. Erevelles, N. & Minear, A. (2010). Unspeakable offenses: Untangling race and disability in discourses of intersectionality. *Journal of literary & cultural disability studies*, 4(2), 127–145. doi:10.3828/jlcds.2010.11.

2   Attention Deficit Hyperactivity Disorder

Melanie Hobbs

PSYCHIATRIST

ⓘ Introduction

Attention Deficit Hyperactivity Disorder, or ADHD, is a **neurodevelopmental** disorder characterised by problems with **attention and/or hyperactivity**.

The prevalence of ADHD in children is around **5%,** while in adults it is around **2.5%** [1].

The Diagnostic and Statistical Manual of Mental Health Disorders (Fifth Edition) [1], which is widely referred to as **DSM-5,-TR** provides a comprehensive list of signs and symptoms that people who have ADHD might complain of. In essence, these signs and symptoms are related to problems with **focus and attention**, moving around more than others **(hyperactivity)** and **impulsive behaviour**.

To be diagnosed with ADHD, these signs and symptoms must have been present for at **least six months**. They also need to occur in **more than one environment** (for example school, home, work) and **negatively influence** a person's life.

There must be symptoms present **before the age of 12** for ADHD to be diagnosed. Parents may notice that their children show some signs of hyperactivity when they are very young, but as most under-fives are similar in this respect, it is unlikely that ADHD would be diagnosed this early. A child with ADHD may have more noticeable difficulties when they enter the school system. Difficulties with attention and hyperactivity can have a negative effect on learning, particularly within a traditional classroom setting.

Symptoms of ADHD tend to remain fairly stable through adolescence and early adulthood, and in about **half of people** [2] with ADHD their difficulties will improve significantly as they get older.

DOI: 10.4324/9781003510659-2

ADHD is generally categorised into **three types** [1, 3]:

- ADHD with a predominance of problems with **attention**
- ADHD with a predominance of **hyperactivity and impulsivity**
- ADHD with equally present symptoms of **both**

It is worth noting that when diagnosing a mental health disorder, the disorder is defined by **the effect that it has on the person** (this is likely to include **distress or impairment** in different areas of life, such as relationships, education and occupation) rather than the effect that it has on people around them.

Often ADHD symptoms are an important part of someone's identity and labelling it as a 'disorder' may feel punitive (especially in children). When someone is being assessed for possible ADHD, it is important to make clear that receiving a diagnosis of ADHD can actually be a **positive experience**. It may lead them to a better understanding and acceptance of themselves. It is also likely to allow them to access specialist help and support, especially in education and employment. The aim of 'management' of ADHD is to help the person have better **control of the symptoms** which cause them difficulty.

This chapter is split up into:

1 Background
2 Heterogeneity within ADHD
3 Things to look out for
4 Screening assessments
5 Specialist assessment
6 Adaptations and considerations
7 Signposting
8 Case examples
9 References

Background

The cause of ADHD (like the cause of most neurodevelopmental and mental health disorders) is not well understood.

There have been many imaging studies of the brains of children with ADHD. These have shown that the cortex in children with ADHD **did not reach peak thickness until several years later** than children who did not have an ADHD diagnosis. The middle prefrontal gyrus was found to have the longest delay in maturation (five years) [4].

A recent area of interest is a circuit in the brain which scientists have named the **'Default Mode Network' (DMN)** [4]. It involves parts of the medial **prefrontal cortex** and posterior **cingulate cortex** and is active when we are not focused on a specific task. In other words, it is our 'Daydreaming Network', which plays an important role in introspection and reflection. The hypothesis is that this **network is overactive** in people with ADHD. Some studies in this area have found that there are **reduced connections** within the circuit in children diagnosed with ADHD compared to the general population [5]. Therefore, it is suggested that due to reduced connections in the DMN people with ADHD find it more difficult to switch off from 'daydreaming mode' and focus on a task.

Other studies have looked at connectivity in the DMN in adults whose ADHD symptoms persisted into adulthood, compared to those who considered themselves to be in 'remission'. They found that adults with continuing ADHD symptoms in adulthood continued to show **reduced connections** in the DMN, whereas adults who had 'grown out' of their ADHD and controls without ADHD were statistically the same [4].

There is ongoing research into other areas of the brain that may be affected, including the **dopaminergic mesolimbic system**, which is hypothesised to be involved in motivation and reward [5].

Whatever the cause, ADHD can cause a huge variety of different challenges, affecting how someone functions in day-to-day life, in school or further education, in the workplace and within their relationships.

Although by definition ADHD is a disorder that emerges in childhood, it **will often go undiagnosed** for many years, sometimes even decades [6]. Parents of adults who present for an assessment for ADHD may explain that they sought help many years earlier but were dismissed by health or educational professionals who told them that their child was simply 'naughty', or that they lacked appropriate parenting skills. There now seems to be an increased awareness of ADHD in education and health professionals, and the general public.

Once diagnosed, there are a wide range of strategies that can help people with ADHD manage the symptoms that distress them.

In **children aged five to eighteen**, the first line recommendation from the National Institute of Clinical Excellence (NICE) [7] is for ADHD focused **parent and/or carer training**. Group-based support is recommended for both parents/carers and young people with ADHD, and NICE recommends this support should include education about ADHD in general, the wider impact it can have on young people's lives and parenting strategies that may be helpful. NICE also recommends getting the young person's school or college involved to discuss how they can support them.

NICE goes on to state that young people should also be offered **Cognitive Behaviour Therapy (CBT)** focussing on social skills, problem-solving, self-control, active listening skills and coping with and expressing feelings.

In adults, NICE recommend that the first step in management of ADHD should be **environmental modifications**. These could include reducing distractions in the workplace by changing seating arrangements, providing headphones to cut out background noise or having short periods of work with 'movement breaks' where employees can get up and walk around [7].

Medication can then be considered if these are not sufficiently helpful [7]. Medication should only be given under specialist supervision (NICE define a specialist as 'a psychiatrist, paediatrician or other appropriately qualified health professional'). The most commonly used medications for ADHD are **methylphenidate, dexamfetamine** and **atomoxetine**. Methylphenidate and dexamfetamine are referred to as 'stimulants', atomoxetine as 'non-stimulant'[2].

All of the medications used for management of ADHD increase the amount of **dopamine** and/or **noradrenaline** in the synaptic space. Their benefit seems to be through action in the **prefrontal cortex** [2].

Table 2.1 below gives more details about the medications licensed for use in people with ADHD in the UK [2].

Table 2.1 Medications licensed for use in people with ADHD in the UK

Medication name	Class	Hypothesised effect on neurotransmitters	Speed of onset
Methylphenidate	Stimulant	Blocks reuptake of noradrenaline and serotonin into the presynaptic neuron.	Fast, but longer acting formulations are also available
Dexamfetamine	Stimulant	Blocks reuptake of noradrenaline and dopamine and increases release into the synaptic space	Very fast acting
Lisdex-amfetamine	Stimulant	Blocks reuptake of noradrenaline and dopamine and increases release into the synaptic space.	Fast (but longer than dexamfetamine)
Atomoxetine	Non-stimulant	Blocks reuptake of noradrenaline by the pre-synaptic noradrenaline transporter	Slow (two to four weeks)

It is worth noting that the **potential for abuse** is high with stimulant medication for ADHD, especially dexamfetamine, due to the fast onset of action. For this reason, dexamfetamine is not licensed for use in adults with ADHD. Instead lisdexamfetamine, a longer-acting formulation of dexamfetamine that is biologically inactive until it is hydrolysed by red blood cells, can be used [2].

Medications for ADHD can lead to various side effects. These include weight loss (generally more problematic in children), increased heart rate and blood pressure and sleep disturbance. People who suffer with **tics** (fast and repeated movement of muscles causing sudden and difficult to control body movements or vocalisations) may find that these increase. There is also an increased risk of **seizures** and **co-morbid mental health problems** (particularly anxiety and psychosis) [2].

Therefore, an important role of the specialist team prescribing medication for ADHD is education about potential side effects. This should involve the person taking the medication and the people they have regular contact with (for example family, friends, carers). Generally, side effects are managed by reducing doses of medication or switching to a different drug [2].

ADHD has been found to be more common in people **with other neurodevelopmental disorders,** particularly autism. Rates of ADHD are also higher in people with **epilepsy, mental health disorders, acquired brain injury** or a history of **substance misuse[7]**.

Having a **family history** of ADHD also makes it more likely [7]. Several studies have attempted to identify the genes responsible, but it seems it is likely to be very complex with multiple genes implicated.

ADHD is also recognised to be found at higher rates in those known to the **criminal justice system** [2]. Therefore, it is important for anyone working with people under the care of neurodevelopmental or mental health services within prison settings to have a good working knowledge of ADHD.

Heterogeneity within ADHD

One area of significant diversity in people with ADHD seems to be between males and females. Rates of **ADHD in boys appear to be around twice as high in girls.** Interestingly, in adults they become more even (1.6:1) [1]. One theory for why this might be is that the persistence of ADHD symptoms into adulthood seems to be around 60% in women, and only 35% in men [8].

Research has shown that **women and girls** have higher rates of problem with **inattention**, and **boys and men** are more likely to show symptoms related to **hyperactivity and impulsivity**. Inattentive symptoms are more likely to persist into adulthood, perhaps explaining why rates in men and women even out as they get older [8].

However, it has also been hypothesised that because females are less likely to present with the most outwardly visible signs of ADHD, there are many girls and women with ADHD who are either **missed** or **mis-diagnosed**. Therefore, it **seems as if rates are higher in males, when in reality they may not be.**

NICE highlight this point in their guidance, reminding clinicians that ADHD is under-recognised in women and girls, leading to a lower rate of referral for assessment and a higher likelihood of receiving an incorrect diagnosis of a different mental health or neurodevelopmental conditions [7].

Another difference between the genders is the rates of co-morbid conditions. Women are more likely to experience **co-morbid depression, anxiety** and **emotional dysregulation,** whilst men with ADHD on the other hand, have higher rates of **substance and alcohol misuse.** One theory for this difference is that men are more likely to externalise and women to internalise the distress caused by ADHD symptoms [8].

It has also been hypothesised that societal and cultural expectations of women make the behaviours associated with ADHD (e.g. impulsivity) less acceptable in women than men. This then leads to self-criticism and low self-esteem, and a higher risk of low mood and anxiety [9].

Studies into rates of diagnosis of ADHD in different cultural groups in America have found **that white children are more likely to be diagnosed with ADHD than black, Hispanic or Asian children** [10]. Reasons for this are poorly understood but are likely to be multifactorial.

A significant area of neurodivergence (which is also discussed in the 'Specialist Assessment' section of this chapter) is autism. There have been several studies into the 'overlap' between ADHD and autism. Research has shown that autistic traits are noted at a higher rate in people with ADHD than the general population [11]. It has also been found that there is a more significant impairment in daily living skills in people with both autism and ADHD than in people with either autism or ADHD as a single diagnosis [11].

(▶) Things to look out for

A helpful way to think about the symptoms of ADHD is to consider each of the categories in DSM-5-TR [1] and the other widely used system, the International Classification of Diseases 11th Revision (ICD-11) [3]: **attention, hyperactivity** and **impulsivity**.

- A person who struggles with sustaining **attention** due to ADHD may find it **hard to concentrate** on something that they do not find stimulating. This can include lessons, meetings, reading and even day to day conversations. They may have **difficulties with school or other academic work**, for example making mistakes due to inattention (such as not following instructions carefully) or not completing work due to being easily distracted.
- They can also have problems with **organisation and time management**, such as not keeping their environment tidy and not meeting deadlines in education or at work. There may also be difficulties with more everyday tasks such as **forgetting** to attend health appointments and not paying bills on time.
  People with ADHD may also be well known for frequently **losing items** that are essential for everyday life, including car keys, mobile phones and wallets.
- With regards to **hyperactivity**, people with ADHD may complain of an **inability to be still**. Friends and family may complain that they are constantly 'fidgeting' and moving around. Being in a situation that involves long periods of sitting, such as classrooms and lecture halls, offices, restaurants or even the cinema can be stressful for someone with ADHD.
- Increased **impulsivity** may mean people with ADHD may make decisions on the **'spur of the moment'** without thinking through possible consequences or **blurt out** opinions without considering their impact. They might find it difficult to **'turn-take'**, for example waiting in a queue in a shop or in traffic can also be challenging.
- **Communication** is another area in which people with hyperactivity and impulsivity in ADHD might struggle. They may talk excessively, interrupt others when talking and 'take over' conversations, which friends and family may find particularly frustrating!
- Sometimes problems are less obvious to the person with ADHD themselves than the people who spend a lot of time with them. For example, friends and family may complain that a person with ADHD does not seem to be listening when they talk to them or is always late for important events. This is why it is important to obtain a collateral history from whoever the person being assessed spends the most time with (parents, partner, friends) to get a full picture of their problems.

Q If carrying out an ADHD assessment for an adult, it is helpful to ask whoever the childhood primary caregiver was for a **developmental history** and to specifically ask if they presented with any of the problems above before the age of 12 years. It can be helpful to start off with an open question like 'Could you tell me more about them as a child?', and then move on to focused questions for example 'Did they often misplace things?' or 'Did their school-teachers report any problems with concentration?'.

Screening assessments

The purpose of a screening tool is to help professionals identify if a person is likely to have ADHD, so they can be referred on for assessment. For example, a GP might ask someone presenting to them to complete assessments, before referring them on to specialist ADHD services within mental health tertiary care.

Screening tools for ADHD are plentiful (a quick internet search will bring up hundreds of sites), but they vary hugely in quality.

The World Health Organisation recommends the **Adult ADHD Self Report Scale** (ASRS-v1.1) for ADHD screening. This comprises of eighteen questions related to common ADHD symptoms, asking the person completing the scale to rate whether they experience them as never, rarely, sometimes, often or very often. The ASRS has been found to have high diagnostic accuracy [12]. It has also been found to have a high sensitivity when used in people with substance use disorders [13].

The Royal College of Psychiatrists [14] recommend that before people are referred for an assessment, they should complete the **Adult ADHD Self Report Scale**, the **Weiss Functional Impairment Rating Scale** and the **10-item Autism Spectrum Quotient**.

The **Weiss Functional Impairment Rating Scale** asks the person completing the tool to rate problems from several different areas – family, work, school, life skills, self-concept, social and risk. The ratings are 0 (never or not at all), 1 (sometimes or somewhat), 2 (often or much) or 3 (very often or very much). The scores can then be added up to give a total in each domain and overall.

The **10-item Autism Spectrum Quotient** is a questionnaire that asks people to rate responses to questions about common issues experienced by autistic individuals. This screening tool is recommended due to the overlap between autism and ADHD which clinicians are becoming increasingly aware of [14].

There are also several recommended tools that specialists may use when diagnosing ADHD, which are included in the section on specialist assessment.

Specialist assessment

Please note that the information in this chapter refers mainly to adults. Most assessments for childhood ADHD are carried out within local paediatric health services or Child and Adolescent Mental Health Services (CAMHS). When assessing children for ADHD there are multiple specialist screening and diagnostic tools available. Input from teachers and professionals such as Occupational and Speech and Language Therapists is also likely to be required.

The **NICE guidelines** for ADHD diagnosis and management [7] state that 'diagnosis should only be made by a specialist **psychiatrist** (mental health doctor), **paediatrician** (doctor who looks after children) or other **appropriately qualified health professional** with training and expertise in the diagnosis of ADHD'. Usually 'other qualified health professionals' who diagnose ADHD are senior nurses with specific experience in certain areas of mental health, or psychologists with a particular interest in ADHD.

It may be helpful to ask patients to complete a self-report scale before they attend for their assessment.

These could include:

- Conner's Adult ADHD Rating Scales
- Current Symptoms Scale (Barkley and Murphy)
- Adult ADHD self-report scale (Kessler et al.)
- ADHD self-report scale (Rosler et al.)
- Copeland Symptom Checklist for Attention Deficit Disorders
- Weiss Functional Impairment Rating Scale
- Current Behavioural Scale – self report (Barkley)

However, it is important to remember that the person has come for an assessment for a disorder of attention. Being overwhelmed with paperwork to fill in may be stressful for them, so limit self-report scales to one or two. The self-report scale can be a useful tool to initiate discussion about symptoms, but it should not be considered a diagnostic tool.

There are several diagnostic tools available for ADHD. One of the most commonly used is the **Diagnostic Interview for ADHD in Adults**, widely referred to as the DIVA. (If you're wondering why DIVA and not DIFA, it is because it was developed by Dutch clinicians, and the name in Dutch was Diagnostisch Interview Voor ADHD.)

The DIVA is easy to find and download online and provides the assessor with questions for a structured interview with the person undergoing assessment. Ideally a person who can give a history of childhood behaviour should also be present as the questions have two components, one relating to current problems and one to childhood.

The Royal College of Psychiatrists [14] also list the **Conners' Adult ADHD Diagnostic Interview for DSM-IV** as a recommended diagnostic tool.

Other widely used tools include the **ADHD Child Evaluation (ACE)** for children aged 5 to 16 years and the **ACE+** (for young people and adults). These were developed by Dr Susan Young and take the form of semi-structured diagnostic interviews. The **Structured Clinical Interview for DSM V (SCID 5-CV)** can also be a helpful assessment tool.

There are various computerised performance tests available, but it is advisable to use these in the context of a component of a holistic assessment and not as a diagnostic tool [15].

Completing an assessment tool can be helpful, but it is only part of the ADHD assessment. To make a diagnosis of ADHD, NICE recommend that a 'full clinical and **psychosocial assessment**' is undertaken [7]. This should include questions about how the person's specific problems affect all aspects of their life, for example work, home and social life. They also recommend taking a **developmental history**, discussing **previous psychiatric problems**, assessing the person's **mental state** and requesting **'observer reports'** (for example from teachers, work colleagues, friends and family). The Royal College of Psychiatrists [14] second this, stating that a thorough **general psychiatric history, developmental history and corroborative history must be taken.**

General psychiatric history should include assessing for symptoms of ADHD and other mental health difficulties, and a Mental State Examination (MSE) should be completed. It is important to establish if there is **family history** of mental health or neurodevelopmental conditions.

Developmental history should be as detailed as possible, in particular around the age of onset of symptoms, and should explore the possibility of **other neurodevelopmental conditions.**

Corroborative history from a caregiver who has known the person since childhood is the gold standard, but if this is not possible then school, higher education or employment records can also be useful. Depending on circumstances, there may also be records from social services or child and adolescent mental health services.

One of the most challenging aspects of completing an assessment for ADHD is being able to **differentiate** it from other mental health difficulties. Often the person may present with a complex picture with lots of different symptoms that may or may not be ADHD related.

For example, a patient with **autism** might present with increased body movements. In autism it is likely the movements will be repetitive or 'stereotypical', for example rocking backwards and forwards, in ADHD they will most likely be described as 'fidgeting' or 'restlessness'.

Anxiety disorders can also present with distractibility and inability to concentrate, but this is generally due to being preoccupied with worries and anxious thoughts. **Depression** may also lead to problems with concentration, but low mood, lack of pleasure from activities they used to enjoy and biological symptoms such as changes to appetite and poor sleep will also be present. They will normally be episodic in nature and not present consistently since childhood like ADHD.

A person with **bipolar disorder** who is suffering from a manic or hypomanic episode may have symptoms of increased energy and impulsivity, such as moving from one 'project' to another without completing any of them. However, in bipolar disorder there will be a predominance of mood symptoms, such as elevated or irritable mood and grandiosity (which can become delusional in nature). Bipolar disorder is also characterised by episodes of mania (or hypomania) and depression, rather than a consistent picture as in ADHD.

Substance misuse, especially those that cause elevated mood and energy, such as amphetamines, may also mimic ADHD. Don't forget to ask about whether the person uses any substances to control their symptoms (sometimes referred to as 'self-medicating'). This can include illicit drugs, but also caffeine (including energy drinks) and nicotine.

Of course, any of the disorders mentioned above can co-exist with ADHD (which is when diagnosis becomes a real challenge!).

The Royal College of Psychiatrists provides a list of rates of comorbidity with other mental health and developmental diagnoses in their ADHD guidelines [14].

- Emotionally unstable personality disorder 13%
- Bipolar affective disorder 20%
- Dysthymia 23%
- Dissocial (or antisocial) personality disorder 24%
- Substance use disorders 25%
- Specific Learning Disability 33%
- Anxiety disorder, up to 33%
- Moderate to severe depressive disorder 63%

It is also thought that there is a **significant overlap with autism [7]**. This is a relatively new area in mental health as it has only recently been possible to diagnose both conditions according to the DSM system for classification. In DSM-IV, which was in use until DSM-5 was published in 2013, a diagnosis of ADHD could not be made if symptoms of inattention and hyperactivity were seen 'exclusively during the course of a pervasive developmental disorder' [13]. However, in DSM-5-TR **it is possible to make a diagnosis of ADHD in the case of an autistic person and vice versa**. Therefore, when taking a developmental history, it is good practice to also ask questions relating to autism as well as ADHD.

The 'gold standard' of an assessment for ADHD is therefore a lengthy assessment, including a developmental history from childhood primary care givers, understanding the current social situation the person finds themselves in, reviewing their psychiatric history and screening for co-morbid mental health problems.

However, it is sometimes the case that large 'chunks' of information are not available to the clinician conducting the assessment. For example, when completing an assessment for a person who is currently in a prison or forensic mental health setting it is often very difficult to obtain a developmental history from family or school records.

The question is then: **can a diagnosis of ADHD be made without this information?**

Different clinicians will have different answers to this question. Some will feel that a diagnosis of ADHD cannot be made without certain pieces of information, some will feel happy to make a 'provisional diagnosis' using their clinical judgement.

A sensible approach can be to inform the person that you have reached the conclusion it is likely they have ADHD, even though you have not been able to complete a full assessment. The pros and cons of a **trial of treatment** (be it psychological, environmental or medical) can then be discussed and the person can make their own decision about how they wish to proceed.

Mental health diagnosis is always based on **clinical judgement alone** as, at the time of writing, we have no reliable biomarkers for any 'non-organic' mental health disorders (e.g. bipolar disorder, depression, schizophrenia). Therefore, the vast majority of clinicians working in mental health will be well used to having to be pragmatic in their approach.

Adaptations and considerations

When assessing someone for ADHD, the following adaptations can be helpful.

✓ Allow plenty of time and be careful not to make the person feel rushed or under pressure.

✓ Minimise possible distractions, such as phones ringing and people chatting outside the room being used.

✓ Make it clear to the person that if they need to, you are happy for them to do what they need to do to feel comfortable, for example getting up and walking around the room or using fidget gadgets.

✓ Be prepared to offer several sessions for an assessment, as it is likely the person may struggle to concentrate for long periods of time.

✓ Try to understand why the person has come for an assessment. Is it primarily to get help at school or in work? Is it because family members have pressured them to attend? Is it because they are really struggling with relationships? This may help you to work with them to meet their specific goals.

✓ Try to get an idea of whether someone would find a diagnosis of ADHD positive or negative. For example, someone people might struggle with being told they have a 'disorder', whilst others may be desperate to work out what is causing them problems and be relieved to be diagnosed with ADHD. This can help you tailor your approach.

✓ Ask the person to attend at least one assessment session with someone who knew them well as a child (generally this will be a parent, but there are many other possible primary caregivers) as this is useful for taking a developmental history.

✓ Ask the person to attend at least one assessment session with someone who spends a lot of time with them now (for example partner/spouse) as they can provide a collateral history.

✓ Provide 'take away' information for them to look at in their own time. Sometimes you might need to think about a different format, for example online videos, as some people with ADHD might find this easier to focus on than written information

✓ Be prepared to repeat conversations and give information several times, as people with ADHD are likely to have difficulty with attention.

✓ When you are confirming and discussing a diagnosis of ADHD it is often helpful for the person to have someone with them in case they later struggle to recall the information that has been provided to them.

✓ Consider the patient's history and current circumstances when prescribing. For example, in people with a history of **substance misuse** you may wish to prescribe atomoxetine, which has a much slower onset of action and therefore lower risk of abuse. There is also a risk of ADHD medication being taken by someone other than the person it is prescribed for (**diversion**) as the stimulant medications have a significant street value. Be vigilant for possible signs of this.

Signposting

NICE suggest that after a person is given a diagnosis of ADHD, they should have the opportunity for a **discussion** with a clinician about what this means for them [7]. Often receiving a diagnosis of ADHD can be a 'relief' and begin a journey towards better understanding and acceptance. For example, for someone who has always criticised themselves for making spur of the moment decisions that have negative consequences, learning they have ADHD may help them to understand why they do this, and what they may be able to do to make a positive change.

This time can be an important opportunity to get **loved ones** involved and explore how ADHD affects behaviour and how this may be perceived or experienced by others. For example, a partner might be frustrated that the person with ADHD has difficulty focusing on their conversations but may be able to understand this better after some learning and reflection about ADHD.

A diagnosis may also open doors to **specialist services**, and additional support at school and other education settings or reasonable adjustment in the workplace.

It is important to know what services are available locally, as this can differ greatly from area to area. This variation has led to ADHD provision being labelled a 'postcode lottery' [16].

Lots of mental health NHS Trusts now have dedicated ADHD teams. However, due to the strain on NHS mental health services their input is often very limited. For example, this often comprises of an assessment, a couple of appointments post diagnosis and then **annual appointments in a specialised medication clinic**, with the person's GP prescribing of medication under a 'shared care agreement'.

Therefore, it is likely the person may have to seek other sources of support.

The Royal College of Psychiatrists [14] recommend the following web-based resources:

- National Attention Deficit Disorder Information and Support Service (ADDiSS) www.addiss.co.uk
- AADD-UK – The site for and by adults with ADHD (aadduk.org)
- ADDers.org

Heather case examples

Heather was a twenty-year-old woman who attended an NHS Specialist ADHD Service assessment appointment with her mother. Heather had presented to her GP as she felt she may have ADHD. Her GP asked her to complete the Adult ADHD Self Report Scale (ASR-v1.1) and, as this screening indicated that ADHD may be relevant to her, she was referred on to secondary services.

The psychiatrist started the assessment by taking a developmental history, asking Heather and her mum what she was like as a child. Mum reported that as a very young child, Heather did not seem much different to her three siblings. She had 'lots of energy' and spent most of her time running around with the other children. As far as her mum could remember Heather hit all her developmental milestones, such as smiling, rolling over, crawling, walking and talking, on time.

She enjoyed school for the first few years as it was mainly learning through play. However, when it came to having lessons which involved sitting at a desk and listening to a teacher she began to struggle. Heather says she remembers one particular teacher who she felt was extra hard on her and would make negative comments about her in front of the rest of the class which used to upset her.

Unfortunately, things at school did not improve as she got older. When she moved to secondary school, she continued to struggle with concentrating in lessons, and she was often accused of 'daydreaming'.

Heather also had difficulties making friends with other children. She states that she did not have great social skills and annoyed others by interrupting them or getting frustrated if she felt they were 'too slow' to do something. Although she desperately wanted a 'best friend', she was never asked by her classmates to do anything outside of school. Luckily, she had her siblings to play with so her mum did not feel this affected her too much.

Heather's mum stated that Heather was quite forgetful as a child, and she was frequently getting calls from school asking her to bring in something that Heather had left behind, e.g. her PE kit. At home, she shared a bedroom with her sister and Heather's side of the room was always messy, with clothes all over the floor. This used to annoy her sister.

When asked about school reports, Heather's mum said that she used to dread Parents' Evening because she was told by most of the teachers that Heather's concentration was poor and that she often seemed uninterested. Interestingly, this never happened in Art, where she always received glowing reports.

Heather was enjoying an art foundation course at college and was hoping to go on to complete an undergraduate degree in an art related topic. Despite her love for the subject, she had struggled in her first term due to not meeting deadlines for assignments. Heather stated that she could focus when she was painting, drawing or sculpting, but when it came to written work she really struggled. This led to her procrastinating and not handing work in on time.

It was actually one of Heather's tutors who had suggested she might have ADHD, as they had a daughter who had recently been diagnosed. Heather had done some research online and the more she had discovered about ADHD, the more she felt it described her.

Heather's mum explained that Heather's dad, with whom they have had very little contact, had lots of similar problems to Heather.

After completing the assessment, it was felt that Heather did have ADHD. She and her mum attended the psychoeducation sessions offered by the Specialist ADHD Service. Heather's tutor helped her to put some changes in place at college such as being given a quieter space to work in. She also put her in contact with Academic Support Services who helped her with improving her organisation and meeting deadlines.

Heather was also offered medication for ADHD, which was commenced by the specialist clinic. Heather found that short acting methylphenidate allowed her to have periods of several hours where her focus improved, and she found it easier to complete written work. Once her dose of medication was stabilised, her ADHD medication was then prescribed by her GP, with Heather attending once yearly appointments at the ADHD service.

Jake case examples

Jake was a 32-year-old man who attended a general psychiatric clinic with his wife Holly. Holly had some concerns about Jake's memory and persuaded him to visit their GP, who referred him for an assessment with secondary mental health services.

Jake worked as a builder for a local company that did fairly small projects, such as home extensions. He reported that he enjoyed the physicality of his work, and the satisfaction in completing his part in a project to a high standard. Jake stated that he would not be suited to a job that involved 'sitting at a desk all day'. He generally got on well with colleagues and customers due to his friendly demeanour and sense of humour.

Jake explained he tried being self-employed for a while, but really struggled with completing paperwork such as sending out invoices to customers and keeping track of payments. Due to this the business suffered financial difficulties and he decided he would rather let someone else 'take care of that side of things'.

Holly and Jake had been together for eight years. Holly said Jake had always had lots of energy, which was one of the things that had drawn her to him. However, now they had children and home life was busier she had become more aware of problems in the relationship. Holly complained that whenever she was talking to Jake, he never seemed to listen. She added that he would often argue with her that she had not told him something when she had. Holly also complained that Jake would often show up late for important events, such as special assemblies at their children's school, despite her reminding him several times. About four months previously he had completely forgotten about Sports Day due to being engrossed in a building job and missed the event altogether, upsetting the children who were expecting to see him there. This had caused a big argument between Jake and Holly. It was in the wake of this incident that Jake agreed to 'see someone' about his memory.

Even though he was an extrovert and enjoyed socialising, if they met up with family or friends Jake would usually end up running around entertaining the kids rather than sitting with the adults and talking.

Holly stated that she enjoyed relaxing on the sofa in the evenings to watch TV when the children were in bed. She said that Jake never sat still for long, and instead of focusing on what they were watching he was always watching videos, playing games or messaging his friends on his phone. He would then ask her a lot of questions about the programme, which irritated her.

When asked about his childhood, Jake stated that he hated school due to finding it difficult to sit still and follow instructions. He joked that he was 'always getting into trouble for messing around'. He reported an overall 'happy childhood' with a loving mum, dad and sister, but did add that his mum used to get annoyed with him over his messy bedroom, and frequently losing things like school jumpers which were expensive to replace.

During the assessment, it seemed that Jake found it difficult to sit still for long. He drummed his fingers on the arm of the chair and shifted position frequently. He also frequently interrupted Holly when she was talking. A couple of times when asked a question, he started answering but went off on a tangent and then stopped to ask, 'What was the question again?'

The assessment took several appointments to complete due to Jake struggling to concentrate for the hour-long session. Jake's mum came to an appointment, where she went through the childhood questions on the DIVA with the clinician and gave a developmental history. Jake and Holly then attended an appointment with the same clinician to complete the questions about current problems.

The clinician was strongly suspicious of ADHD and referred to the Specialist ADHD Service who completed their assessment. The outcome was that Jake was diagnosed with ADHD. Holly and Jake attended some joint appointments with the service's psychologist and discussed the diagnosis and how it was affecting their relationship.

Jake considered medication for ADHD but decided that he did not wish to pursue this. Instead, he worked with Holly to build a plan to help him remember appointments and events (including mobile phone diary alerts and alarms).

Jake felt that these changes improved his organisation skills, which also helped his relationship with Holly and their children. Holly found attending a support group for family members of people with ADHD gave her a better understanding of Jake's behaviour and she found herself becoming less sensitive to the behaviours that had previously caused tension between them.

References

1. American Psychiatric Association. (2013). *Diagnostic and Statistical Manual of Mental Disorders* (5th ed.). American Psychiatric Association.
2. Johnson, J., Morris, S., & George, S. (2020). Attention deficit hyperactivity disorder in adults: What the non-specialist needs to know. *British Journal of Hospital Medicine*, 8(3). doi:10.12968/hmed.2019.0188.
3. World Health Organisation. (2022). *International Classification of Diseases* (11th Revision). World Health Organisation.
4. Jadidian, A., Hurley, R. A., & Taber, K. H. (2015). Neurobiology of adult ADHD: Emerging evidence for network dysfunctions. *Journal of Neuropsychiatry Clinical Neuroscience*, 27(3), 173–178. doi:10.1176/appi.neuropsych.15060142.
5. Posner, J., Polanczyk, G. V., & Sonuga-Barke, E. (2020). Attention-deficit hyperactivity disorder. *Lancet*, 395(10222), 450–462. doi:10.1016/S0140-6736(19)33004-1.

6. Oliva, F., Malandrone, F., Mirabella, S., Ferreri, P., di Girolamo, G., & Maina, G. (2021). Diagnostic delay in ADHD: Duration of untreated illness and its socio-demographic and clinical predictors in a sample of adult out-patients. *Early Intervention in Psychiatry*, 15(4), 957–965. doi:10.1111/eip.13041.

7. National Institute for Health and Care Excellence. (2024). Attention Deficit Hyperactivity Disorder clinical knowledge summary. Scenario: Management of attention deficit hyperactivity disorder (ADHD). Retrieved from https://cks.nice.org.uk/topics/attention-deficit-hyperactivity-disorder/management/management/.

8. Stibbe, T., Huang, J., Paucke, M., Ulke, C., & Strauss, M. (2020). Gender differences in adult ADHD: Cognitive function assessed by the test of attentional performance. *PLoS ONE*, 15(10). doi:10.1371/journal.pone.0240810.

9. Attoe, D. & Climie, E. (2023) Miss. diagnosis: A systematic review of ADHD in adult women. *Journal of Attention Disorders*, 27(2), 645–657. doi:10.1177/10870547231161533.

10. Shi, Y., Guevara, L. R. H., Dykoff, H. J., Sangaralingham, L. R., Phelan, S., Zaccaiello, M. J., & Warner, D. O. (2021). Racial disparities in diagnosis of Attention-Deficit/Hyperactivity disorder in a US national birth cohort. *JAMA Network Open*, 4(3). doi:10.1001/jamanetworkopen.2021.0321.

11. Craig, F., Lamanna, A. L., Margari, F., Matera, E., Simone, M., & Margari, L. (2014). Overlap between autism spectrum disorders and Attention Deficit Hyperactivity Disorder: Searching for distinctive/common clinical features. *Autism Research*, 8(3), 328–337. doi:10.1002/aur.1449.

12. Brevik, E., Lundervold, A. J., Haavik, J., & Posserud, M-B. (2020). Validity and accuracy of the Adult Attention-Deficit/Hyperactivity Disorder (ADHD) Self-Report Scale (ASRS) and the Wender Utah Rating Scale (WURS) symptom checklists in discriminating between adults with and without ADHD. *Brain and Behaviour* 10(6). doi:10.1002/brb3.1605.

13. Van de Glind, G., van den Brink, W., Koeter, M. W. J., Carpentier, P-J., van Emmerik-van Ootmerssen, K., Kaye, S., Skutle, A., Bu, E-T. H., Franck, J., Konstenius, M., Moggi, F., Dom, G., Verspreet, S., Demetrovics, Z., Kapitany-Foveny, M., Fatseas, M., Auriacombe, M., Schillinger, A., Seitz, A., ... & Levin F. R. (2013). Validity of the Adult ADHD Self-Report Scale (ASRS): a short screening scale for use in the general population. *Psychological Medicine* 35(2), 245–256. doi:10.1016/j.drugalcdep.2013.04.010.

14. Royal College of Psychiatrists in Scotland. (2017). ADHD in adults: good practice guideline s. Retrieved from: https://www.rcpsych.ac.uk/docs/default-source/members/divisions/scotland/adhd_in_adultsfinal_guidelines_june2017.pdf.

15. Arrondo, G., Mulraney, M., Iturmendi-Sabater, I., Musullulu, H., Gambra, L., Niculcea, T., Banascheqski, T., Simonoff, E., Dopfner, M., Hinshaw, S. P., Coghill, D., & Cortese, S. (2024). Systematic review and meta-analysis: Clinical utility of continuous performance tests for the identification of Attention-Deficit/Hyperactivity Disorder. *Journal of the American Academy of Child and Adolescent Psychiatry*, 63(2), 154–171. doi:10.1016/j.jaac.2023.03.011.

16. Young, S., Asherson, P., Lloyd, T., Absoud, M., Arif, M., Colley, W. A., Cortese, A., Cubbin, S., Doyle, N., Dunn Morua, S., Ferreira-Lay, P., Gud-jonsson, G., Ivens, V., Jarvis, C., Lewis, A., Mason, P., Newlove-Delgado, T., Pitts, M., Read, H., ... & Skirrow, C. (2001) Failure of healthcare provision for Attention-Deficit/Hyperactivity Disorder in the United Kingdom: A consensus statement. *Frontiers in Psychiatry, 19(*12). doi:10.3389/fpsyt.2021.649399.

3 Autism

Hannah Carton

FORENSIC PSYCHOLOGIST

Introduction

A brief note on language prior to the commencement of this chapter:
for the most part this chapter will use neuro-affirmative language for
autism, however there will be times when medicalised language is
used as a reflection of the current predominant narrative.

Autism is a neurotype[1] shared by up to 3% of the population [1]. Within
medical and diagnostic settings, it is most often referred to as Autism
Spectrum Disorder (ASD), or more recently as Autism Spectrum
Condition (ASC). Whilst the term autism is preferred within autistic
communities, and thus also within a neuro-affirmative approach, it is
important to be familiar with other descriptors as it is likely that you will
come across these in both clinical practice and research.

Autism affects the ways that individuals process, perceive, communicate,
and interact with the world around them. Whilst characteristics and
presentations vary there are core features of autism, including: **differences
in reciprocal social interaction, preferences for specific/repeated movements,
need for specific routines/thinking patterns, particular passions, or interests;
and different sensory experiences.** These characteristics are present across
multiple contexts, commence in early development, and persist over the
lifespan. Whilst autism is a single diagnosis there is a vast amount of
variety within this, such that autism is understood on a spectrum. Autism
is defined using these behaviourally based criteria because, thus far, there
are no known biological markers [2].

There are an estimated 700,000 children and adults diagnosed with
autism in the UK (that is approximately 1% of the population) so it is
likely that either as a clinician or in your day-to-day life you will know

DOI: 10.4324/9781003510659-3

an autistic person [3]. It is reported that approximately 32% of people diagnosed with a Learning Disability (LD) are also diagnosed with autism [4]. Although the figure of 700,000 is widely used when discussing prevalence rates of autism in the UK, it has been estimated that this could be as high as 1.2 million if the number of undiagnosed autistic people were also included. O'Nions et al. (2023) [1] suggest that as of 2018, 463,500 people (0.82% of the English population) may have been diagnosed with autism, and between 435,700 and 1,197,300 people may be autistic and undiagnosed (59%–72% of autistic people, 0.77%–2.12% of the English population).

Currently, within clinical settings, autism is predominantly spoken about using language rooted in the medical model; this chapter promotes viewing autism through the lens of acknowledging variation within **neurodiversity**. Neurodiversity is a neutral word used to explain variety within the human brain, similar to the use of biodiversity to explain the variations in life on earth. **Neurodivergent**[2] is the term used to describe those whose brains diverge significantly from the 'norm' of a given society. Key texts used within the medical approach to autism (ICD-11 [5] and DSM-5-TR [6]) describe 'persistent deficits' or 'impairments' in various areas as core to their diagnostic criteria. This can have the consequence of placing focus on what those individuals with a diagnosis of autism cannot do, rather than where their strengths lie.

Table 3.1 below shows the current diagnostic criteria for autism within both the ICD-11 and DSM-5-TR. The definition of autism has changed many times over the years and is likely to continue to change with growing understanding (please see the *Background* section for more details on the development of our understanding of autism). Both the ICD-11 and the DSM-5-TR set out specific criteria for diagnosing autism (these criteria are then used to inform screening and diagnostic tools).

Whilst it is likely that these manuals will remain the primary guides for diagnosing autism it is important to ensure that we are conscious of the deficits-based language used within them and ensuring that we maintain a neuro-affirmative stance in our own reporting. One way to do this is to reframe autism from a deficient based disorder to a distinct neurotype; that is a naturally occurring brain difference leading to a different way of experiencing the world.

Examples of language shift from deficit based to neuro-affirmative:

Disorder → Difference
Symptoms → Characteristics
Treatment → Support/accommodations

Table 3.1 ASD diagnosis in the ICD-11 and DSM-5-TR

Diagnostic manual	Description
ICD-11 for Mortality and Morbidity Statistics (World Health Organisation; 2021) CODE: 6A02	Autism spectrum disorder is characterised by persistent deficits in the ability to initiate and to sustain reciprocal social interaction and social communication, and by a range of restricted, repetitive, and inflexible patterns of behaviour, interests or activities that are clearly atypical or excessive for the individual's age and sociocultural context. The onset of the disorder occurs during the developmental period, typically in early childhood, but symptoms may not become fully manifest until later, when social demands exceed limited capacities. Deficits are sufficiently severe to cause impairment in personal, family, social, educational, occupational or other important areas of functioning and are usually a pervasive feature of the individual's functioning observable in all settings, although they may vary according to social, educational, or other context. Individuals along the spectrum exhibit a full range of intellectual functioning and language abilities.
Diagnostic and Statistical Manual of Mental disorders; Fifth Edition (DSM-5-TR; American Psychiatric Association, 2022) CODE: 299.00 (F84.0)	A. Persistent deficits in social communication and social interaction across multiple contexts, as manifested by all of the following, currently or by history (examples are illustrative, not exhaustive; see text): 1. Deficits in social-emotional reciprocity, ranging, for example, from abnormal social approach and failure of normal back-and-forth conversation; to reduced sharing of interests, emotions, or affect; to failure to initiate or respond to social interactions. 2. Deficits in nonverbal communicative behaviours used for social interaction, ranging, for example, from poorly integrated verbal and nonverbal communication; to abnormalities in eye contact and body language or deficits in understanding and use of gestures; to a total lack of facial expressions and nonverbal communication. 3. Deficits in developing, maintaining, and understanding relationships, ranging, for example, from difficulties adjusting behaviour to suit various social contexts; to difficulties in sharing imaginative play or in making friends; to absence of interest in peers. Specify current severity: Severity is based on social communication impairments and restricted, repetitive patterns of behaviour (see Table 3.2).

Diagnostic manual	Description
	B. Restricted, repetitive patterns of behaviour, interests, or activities, as manifested by at least two of the following, currently or by history (examples are illustrative, not exhaustive; see text):
	1. Stereotyped or repetitive motor movements, use of objects, or speech (e.g., simple motor stereotypes, lining up toys or flipping objects, echolalia, idiosyncratic phrases).
	2. Insistence on sameness, inflexible adherence to routines, or ritualized patterns of verbal or nonverbal behaviour (e.g., extreme distress at small changes, difficulties with transitions, rigid thinking patterns, greeting rituals, need to take same route or eat same food every day).
	3. Highly restricted, fixated interests that are abnormal in intensity or focus (e.g., strong attachment to or preoccupation with unusual objects, excessively circumscribed or perseverative interests).
	4. Hyper- or hypo-reactivity to sensory input or unusual interest in sensory aspects of the environment (e.g., apparent indifference to pain/temperature, adverse response to specific sounds or textures, excessive smelling or touching of objects, visual fascination with lights or movement). Specify current severity: Severity is based on social communication impairments and restricted, repetitive patterns of behaviour.
	C. Symptoms must be present in the early developmental period (but may not become fully manifest until social demands exceed limited capacities or may be masked by learned strategies in later life).
	D. Symptoms cause clinically significant impairment in social, occupational, or other important areas of current functioning.
	E. These disturbances are not better explained by intellectual disability (intellectual developmental disorder) or global developmental delay. Intellectual Disability and Autism Spectrum Disorder frequently co-occur; to make comorbid diagnoses of Autism Spectrum Disorder and Intellectual Disability, social communication should be below that expected for general developmental level.

As mentioned above, autism is understood on a spectrum and as such not all autistic people will require the same level of support in the same areas (nor will they require the same level of support at different stages of their lives). The DSM-5-TR uses specifiers relating to autism; one of these specifiers is 'severity'. There are three levels of severity: level one, requiring support, level two, requiring substantial support and level three, requiring very substantial support.

This chapter is divided into the following sections:

1   Background
2   Heterogeneity within autism
3   Things to look out for
4   Screening assessments
5   Specialist assessment
6   Adaptations and considerations
7   Signposting
8   Case example
9   References

Background

As was mentioned in the introduction to this chapter, the definition of autism has been through many iterations. Below is a chronology of the key events leading to the current understanding of autism.

Whilst it is important to understand the history of autism and its presentation, it is of equal importance to be aware of the current key documents which relate to autism in the UK:

- **The Autism Act 2009** was the first disability-specific piece of legislation in England. This act aimed to improve the lives of autistic adults and their families by ensuring that the government introduced and regularly reviews an **Adult Autism Strategy**. This Act aimed to address the multitude of social disadvantages and health and care inequalities experienced by autistic adults.
- In 2021 the government published **The National Strategy for Autistic Children, Young People and Adults: 2021 to 2026**. This strategy replaced the previous strategies **'Think Autism' (2014)** and **'Fulfilling and Rewarding Lives' (2010)**, and is the first autism strategy to include children as well as adults. This strategy focuses on autism awareness for the general public, access to education and employment, improving health and care, reducing inpatient care and

Table 3.2 Timeline of our understanding of autism

Year	Key events	Impact from a neuro-affirmative perspective
1908	**Eugene Bleuler** uses the term 'autism' to describe some symptoms of schizophrenia. Autism in this context referring to a retreat to an inner world and an avoidance of reality.	Began the medicalised view of autism as a form of 'childhood schizophrenia' and thus that this was something which could be 'recovered from'.
1943	**Leo Kanner** uses the term 'Infantile Autism' to describe a pattern of behaviour in children including problems with social interaction and a need for sameness. Kanner concluded that Infantile Autism was a neurodevelopmental condition.	
1944	**Hans Asperger** reported on boys who had noticeable difficulties in social interaction, unusual and specific interests, and good verbal skills. This group of traits was to become Asperger's syndrome. Recognition of the genetic component of autism.	Hans Asperger worked with a doctor named **Erwin Lazar** who did not view autistic children as sick but rather that they were affected by a society that was unable to cater to their unique learning style.
1967	**Bruno Bettelheim** published 'The empty fortress', proposing that childhood autism was the result of maternal inadequacy and emotional absence. Key recommendation for autistic children became institutionalisation.	These views were widely accepted by the medical community leading to stigma around autism and blame placed on mothers.
1978	**Michael Rutter** proposes a definition of autism which includes delayed and deviant social and language abilities beyond general developmental level, restricted interests and repetitive behaviours, all with onset early in life.	
1979	**Lorna Wing** and **Judith Gould** examined the prevalence of autism, as defined by Leo Kanner, among children known to have special needs. They found that a large number of the children did not fit the full picture of autism, and they were described as being 'on the autism spectrum'.	Highlighted the vast variability in autistic individuals.

Year	Key events	Impact from a neuro-affirmative perspective
1980	Autism is included in the DSM-III as a pervasive developmental disorder. Criteria were outlined for the diagnosis of autism, including a lack of interest in people, severe impairments in communication, and bizarre responses to the environment, all developing in the first 30 months of life.	
1987	The DSM-III is revised and the criteria for diagnosing autism are altered to broaden the concept of autism to include milder presentation, and no longer requiring development prior to 30 months of age. **Ivar Lovaas** begins studying intensive behaviour therapy for autistic children, known as ABA.	Maintaining the narrative that behaviours displayed by autistic people are undesirable and need to be changed.
1992	Asperger's syndrome is included as a diagnosis in the ICD-10.	
1994	The DSM-IV revises the diagnosis of autism again, now including Asperger's syndrome as a separate subcategory.	Diagnostic rates for autism increased; this led to a discussion of autism diagnosis being labelled an epidemic.
1998	**Andrew Wakefield** publishes an article suggesting that the MMR vaccine was linked with the increase in diagnosis of autism.	Another block in the development of our understanding of autism.
2013	The DSM-5 combines all subcategories of autism into one diagnosis: 'autism spectrum disorder'.	

increasing community support, and improving support within the criminal justice system.

- The **NHS Long Term Plan (2019)** includes goals for improving access to diagnosis and post-diagnostic support as well as specific actions for tackling preventable deaths for autistic people.
- The **NICE Quality Standards on Autism (QS51; 2014)** covers health and social care services for autistic adults, young people and children. It includes information on quality standards relating to assessment and diagnosis of autism, and care and support for people diagnosed with autism.

- The **NICE Clinical Guidelines on autism spectrum disorder in adults: diagnosis and management (CG142; 2021)** covers diagnosing and managing suspected or confirmed autism in people aged 18 and over. It aims to improve access and engagement with interventions and services, and the experience of care, for people with autism.

Heterogeneity within autism

Autism does not discriminate; it affects people of all ages, races, ethnicities, genders, and social status equally. Research indicates that autism appears to be under-investigated, under-recognised, misdiagnosed or diagnosed late in many vulnerable and/or disadvantaged groups [7]. Reasons for this may include healthcare professional bias (exacerbated by biases inherent in diagnostic tools), language differences, social stigma, and varying cultural norms. In order to ensure that we are taking an **intersectional approach**[3] to understanding autism, clinicians must place importance on understanding the differences within autism.

The prevalence of autism has increased over the last decade, however most estimations regarding prevalence rates come from developed, Western countries. There is no reliable and consistent data from non-Western and non-affluent countries [8].

> **Note: Masking** (also known as camouflaging) in autism is the conscious or subconscious process of changing or concealing natural autistic characteristics in order to 'fit in', or as a survival strategy. **Masking, compensation,** and **assimilation** are all forms of masking [9]. Masking refers to the strategies used to conceal autistic characteristics and portray a neurotypical façade (e.g. forcing eye contact, supressing natural body movements); compensation refers to the strategies used to actively compensate for difficulties in social situations (e.g. mimicking body language and facial expressions); and assimilation refers to the strategies used to try to fit in with others in social situations (e.g. maintaining a social interaction beyond the point of enjoyment). Compensatory strategies such as these can be used by any autistic person but may be of particular relevance when considering the intersection of gender and autism.

Age

Autism is predominantly diagnosed in childhood (although an ever-increasing number of adults are seeking diagnosis). Because of this autism is often perceived as a 'childhood disorder'. There is very little known about the process of ageing with autism. Clinicians face challenges in identifying autistic characteristics in older adults, especially in the ways these may differ from the characteristics shown by a younger autistic individual. This is likely due to an older adult's need to have developed various masking strategies over time to survive, resulting in undiagnosed older adults failing to be identified by social or healthcare services [10].

O'Nions et al. (2023) [1] use a sample of 602,433 individuals registered at an English primary care practice in 2018, and 5,586,100 individuals registered between 2000 and 2018 to assess underdiagnosis of autism. Rates of diagnosed autism in children were much higher than in adults and older adults. They found that 2.94% of 10- to 14-year-olds had a diagnosis (1 in 34), vs. 0.02% aged 70+ (1 in 6,000).

Sex and gender[4]

Historically, autism has been understood to be more prevalent in men. The first set of characteristics of autism published by Kanner and Asperger (1943, 1944) were formed within the medical model on a sample made up primarily of young boys. As a result of this, autistic women often do not fit the diagnostic criteria or do not present in a way that professionals are expecting and, as such, diagnosis is delayed or missed entirely. Overall, less research and clinical time has gone into understanding the presentation of autism in women and girls. Brown et al., 2020 [11] reported that autism was diagnosed at a ratio of approximately three males to one female.

It is known that differences in social communication or social interaction are less frequently observed in autistic women than autistic men, it is thought that this may to be due to autistic women's abilities to mask. This can lead to women scoring highly on self-report measures of autistic traits but being overlooked during observation-based testing.

Many autistic women are first diagnosed with Borderline Personality Disorder[5] (BPD) or anxiety disorders due to overlap in areas such as understanding and explaining their emotions, self-injury, intense relationships/friendships and challenges in social functioning.

It is important to note that existing screening and diagnostic assessment have been normed on predominantly male samples, creating a male-biased diagnostic process. As such women and girls are less likely to receive a diagnosis based solely on the standardised tools. Therefore, there continues to be a need to develop and/or adapt the currently available screening tools and diagnostic instruments to improve the identification of autistic women [12].

Race and ethnicity

De Leeuw et al. (2020) [13] have reported that whilst the broad domains of autism diagnosis are universally relevant among autistic individuals, cultural differences may become apparent in expression of characteristics. For example, the degree of eye contact expected in Western cultures differs from that expected in Chinese culture where a child making eye contact with an adult can be considered impolite. Similarly, differences may be apparent in whether these characteristics cause 'significant impairment' to functioning. The impact of certain communication differences may vary between someone who works from home and someone whose occupation requires them to socialise and engage with others on a daily basis.

There is a lack of research regarding the experience of autistic people from Black, Asian and Minority Ethnic (BAME) groups. This in turn can mean that it is harder for individuals from BAME communities to get the support that they need. Mandell et al. (2024) [14] report that in their sample of 406 children, African-American children were 2.6 times less likely than white children to be diagnosed with autism.

The National Autistic Society (NAS[6]) reported that autistic people from BAME communities are less likely to be diagnosed, receive benefits, and access appropriate service.

Social disadvantage

People of low socio-economic status are often at an increased risk of many physical and mental health conditions. However, an opposite pattern is often noted for children with autism, whereby rates of diagnosis are greatly increased in higher socio-economic status societies [15]. Parents or individuals from more affluent areas are more likely to be more aware of the traits of autism and more likely to be in closer proximity to services [8].

There may be several reasons why recognising and diagnosing autism may be more difficult in certain individuals:

- Differences in cultural understanding of autism.
- Inaccurate assumptions about language abilities and behaviours.

- Perceived as a condition affecting white people [7].
- Patients and caregivers from different ethnic groups may describe their experiences differently to healthcare professionals, impacting on the likelihood that such features are deemed consistent with a diagnosis of autism [16].
- Levels of understanding of autism differ between communities.
- Lack of interpreter/translation services to accompany autism services.
- Gendered assumptions regarding the observable presentation of autism and who it impacts.
- Increased masking utilised by women and girls.
- Characteristics of autism misattributed to other mental health conditions.
- Standardised assessments which do not account for the presentation of characteristics in diverse populations.
- Lack of awareness and understanding of autism in adults on the part of healthcare professionals.
- Older adults may be less likely to view themselves as autistic and therefore not come forward for diagnostic assessment.
- Milder or harder to recognise features meaning that potential autism was not picked up during childhood.
- Adults may have developed skills in masking or hiding their autistic characteristics over time.
- It can be harder to obtain a developmental history from family members for adults either due to the amount of time that has elapsed since the individual was a baby or the absence of a parental figure who can provide this information.

Things to look out for

Autism effects the ways that individuals process, perceive, communicate, and interact with the world around them. There are a number of core features of autism, all of which carry with them areas to look out for as a clinician.

Neurodevelopmental disorders frequently co-occur. For example, individuals with autism often have Learning Disability (LD) or Attention-Deficit Hyperactivity Disorder (ADHD). Please see chapters relating to these conditions for further information.

When looking out for characteristics of autism it is important to keep **diagnostic overshadowing**[7] in mind. Diagnostic overshadowing is often attributed to the missed diagnosis of individuals with autism, as characteristics of autism can be overshadowed by characteristics of

Experiences of reciprocal social interaction

- Communication preferences: e.g. written versus face-to-face communication, processing speed
- Interaction preferences: e.g. small groups or one-on-one
- Conversation style: e.g. topics, small-talk
- Sharing of passions/ emotions/affect
- Experience of relationships: e.g. understanding, initiating, maintaining social interactions
- Experience of non-spoken communication: e.g. body language, facial expressions, gesture

Preferences for passions, or interests specific/repeated movements, need for specific routines/thinking patterns, particular

- Particular or repeated motor movements: e.g. rocking, pacing, finger tapping, fidgeting
- Use of objects or vocalisations to regulate
- Preferences for routines
- Experience of change, transitions, thinking patterns
- Passions and interests for specific topics or activities

Sensory experiences

- Auditory: e.g. volume, type of noise, sounds
- Tactile: e.g. light/deep touch, clothing, pain, textures
- Visual: e.g. clutter, light
- Olfactory e.g strong smells
- Gustatory: e.g. types of food
- Vestibular: e.g. dizziness, movement, body sensations
- Proprioception: e.g. personal space, body position
- Interoception: e.g. body signals, emotional states
- Over or under responsivity to sensory stimuli
- Sensory seeking

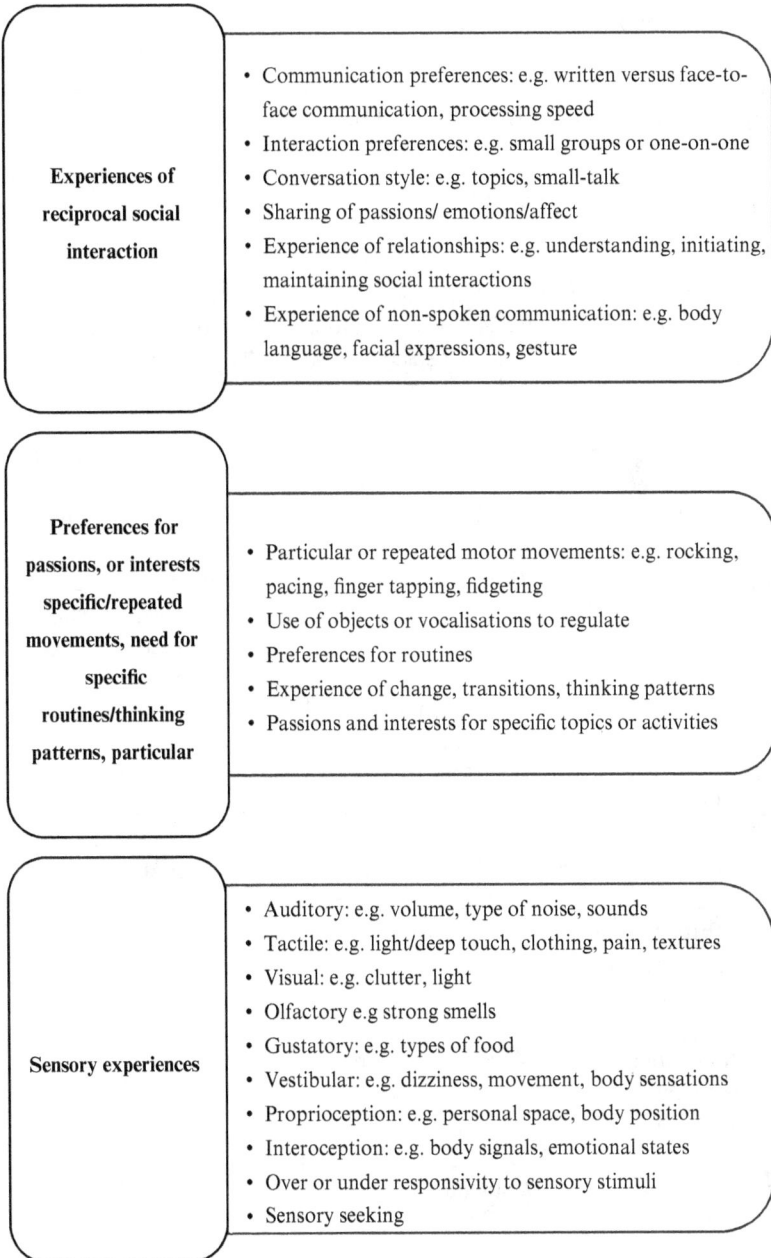

Figure 3.1 Core features of autism

other conditions such as ADHD, anxiety, depression, or LD [15]. For example, differences in social communication can often present as an anxiety disorder, or restricted, repetitive behaviours or interest as obsessive-compulsive disorder[8] (OCD).

Screening assessments

> **Note:** Hold in mind that the imbalance of our understanding on the presentation of autism has an ongoing impact on the referral for autism assessment as well as the screening and diagnostic assessments used.

The first step in both screening and specialist autism assessment is ensuring accessibility. This may mean ensuring that the environment can accommodate for different sensory and support needs: dim the lights, block out excessive noise, smells, adjust temperature, reduce visual input, use an optional chaperone, monitor with feedback.

Evaluation and support are important for autistic people. For example, establishing a formal diagnosis may enable access to social and medical services/pathways if needed. A diagnostic explanation may help an individual and their family understand their differences better and enable community connections. A diagnosis can also lead to reasonable adjustments for that individual within education or employment, for example.

Below are presented several tools which can be used in the screening of potential autism. Whilst screening tools are useful for aiding understanding of an individual, often the language within them conforms to the medical model understanding of autism. It is necessary therefore that if you are using assessments such as these, that interpretation is made in line with a neuro-affirmative approach.

> **Note:** Screening tools alone should not be used to determine whether someone should progress through to a full assessment or not.

- **Adult Repetitive Behaviours Questionnaire-3 (RBQ-3; Leekam & Jones, 2019)**

    a   Self- or informant-report questionnaire that measures repeated behaviours in adults or children.

- **AQ-10 Autism Spectrum Quotient (Allison et al., 2012)**

  a Self-report questionnaire most widely used by primary healthcare professionals as step one in referral for autism assessment.

- **Autism Spectrum Quotient (AQ; Baron-Cohen et al., 2001)**

  a Self-report questionnaire to measure autistic characteristics in adults without LD.

- **Autism Spectrum Screening Questionnaire (ASSQ; Ehlers et al., 1999)**

  a Assessment completed by caregivers or teachers of children or adolescents (6-to-17-years-old).

- **Autism Spectrum Screening Questionnaire (ASSQ-REV; Kopp & Gillberg, 2011)**

  a An extension of the ASSQ for use with girls.

- **Camouflaging Autistic Traits Questionnaire (CAT-Q; Hull et al. 2018)**

  a Self-report measure of social masking behaviours in adults. It may be used to identify autistic individuals who do not currently meet diagnostic criteria due to their ability to mask their autistic traits.
  b Designed for use with adults without LD.

- **Childhood Autism Rating Scale (CARS2; Schopler et al., 2010)**

  a Brief rating scale that helps identify autism in children.

- **Empathy Quotient (EQ; Baron-Cohen and Wheelwright, 2004)**

  a Self-report questionnaire designed to measure empathy in adults.

- **Girls Questionnaire for Autism Spectrum Condition (GQ-ASC; Brown et al., 2020)**

  a Self-report questionnaire designed to identify behaviours and abilities in women that are associated with autism.

- **Multidimensional Assessment of Interoceptive Awareness – Version 2 (MAIA-2; Mehling et al., 2018)**

  a   Self-report questionnaire to measure multiple dimensions of interoception (awareness of bodily sensations).

- **Ritvo Autism Asperger Diagnostic Scale–Revised (RAADS–R; Ritvo et al., 2011)**

  a   Self-report questionnaire designed to identify autistic adults who may be missed for diagnosis due to their presentation.

- **Social Communication Questionnaire (SCQ; Bailey & Lord, 2003)**

  a   Caregiver-report screening of symptoms associated with autism.
  b   Two forms are available, *Current*, which looks at the child's last 3 months, and *Lifetime*, which looks at the child's entire developmental history.

- **Social Responsiveness Scale, Second Edition (SRS-2; Constantino, 2012)**

  a   Identifies the presence of social communication differences and assists in differential diagnosis of this.

- **Systemizing Quotient–Revised (SQ–R; Wheelwright et al., 2006)**

  a   Self-report questionnaire, which is used to assess systemizing cognitive styles. Systemizing is the drive to analyse or construct systems.

Specialist assessment

Helpful Reading: Hartman, D., O'Donnell-Killen, T., Doyle, J. K., Kavanagh, M., Day, A., & Azevedo, J. (2023). *The Adult Autism Assessment Handbook: A Neurodiversity Affirmative Approach.* Jessica Kingsley Publishers.

Note: There are no biomarkers for autism, therefore there are no specific physical tests or scans for autism. As such **autism is a clinical**

diagnosis based on observable behaviour, clinical interview and historical reports. It is also important to note that the diagnostic process for autism is ever evolving and that a neuro-affirmative approach to this is relatively new. This section will outline two potential specialist assessment processes, one which promotes a collaborative assessment framework and one which utilises formal, standardised assessment procedures.

Prior to commencing an assessment for autism remember that the current system is deficit-based so there is a need for assessors working in a neuro-affirmative manner to consult the language they are using during assessment and reporting and ensuring that they are placing the individual's history, experiences, thoughts, and feelings the forefront of assessment.

Collaborative assessment framework

A neuro-affirmative approach to diagnostic assessment ensures that the central component to the process is the individual feeling supported in exploring their identity and the ways in which their inner experiences relate to this. This assessment process is collaborative and emphasises autistic strengths through making sense of the individual's life experiences. This neuro-affirmative assessment framework ensures that all areas identified within the broad domains of the autistic criteria are discussed and aligned with the individual's sense of self. It is important to make sure that this process remains multi-disciplinary in nature and that other professionals are consulted (e.g. Occupational Therapist, Speech and Language Therapist, Psychiatrist).

Standardised assessment procedure

The NICE clinical guidance for the diagnosis and management of autism states that '*when the diagnostic assessment process works well, professionals, the autistic person and their family, partner or carer(s) communicate right from the start and the autistic person is involved in the decisions relating to their care*' [17]. It outlines that a comprehensive assessment should be undertaken by competent and trained professionals, be multidisciplinary team-based and (ideally) involve someone known to the person.

Information about differences in social communication, interaction, behaviours and interests and sensory experiences must be collected in a systematic way. Where possible, information concerning the individual's developmental history should be gathered from a source close to the individual (e.g. a parent or guardian). A clinical history must also be obtained from the individual themselves.

There are various ways in which to conduct a diagnostic assessment for autism. However, guidance published in the National Framework to Deliver Improved Outcomes in All-Age Autism Assessment Pathways: Guidance for Integrated Care Boards (2023) noted that standard assessments should include: a clinical interview, behavioural observation, integration of developmental and corroborative information, use of validated assessment tools, a broader assessment of clinical presentation, and consideration of possible differential and co-occurring diagnoses [18]. This can be completed by one or more appropriately qualified clinician(s).

There are a number of tools which can be used in the diagnosis of autism:

- **Autism Clinical Interview Adults (ACIA)**

  a   Semi-structured interview designed for use as part of a multi-disciplinary diagnostic process for adults.
  b   The interview provides a framework for developmental history.
  c   Available in two versions: subject and informant.

- **Autism Diagnostic Interview – Revised (ADI-R)**

  a   Extended, semi-structured interview of a parent or caregiver who is knowledgeable about the individual's behaviour, development, and functioning currently and in the past, focusing on the period from 4 to 5 years old.

- **Autism Diagnostic Observation Schedule (ADOS-2)**

  a   Standardised assessment tool.
  b   Semi-structured evaluation that measures communication, social interaction, play, and repeated behaviours.
  c   Involves interview and imaginative play.
  d   Only looks at current presentation of behaviour and skill.
  e   Can be used with children, young people and adults with varying levels of cognitive and verbal ability.

- **Developmental, Dimensional and Diagnostic Interview (3Di)**

  a   Computer based interview used to diagnose autism in children.

b   Matches the ADI-R algorithms but is focused largely on current rather than historical behaviour of note.

- **Diagnostic Interview for Social and Communication Disorders (DISCO)**

  a   Detailed, semi-structured interview designed to find out about a person's development, behaviour, and skills from birth through to the present day.
  b   Can be used with children, young people and adults with varying levels of cognitive ability.
  c   Can help to identify comorbid conditions.

- **Monteiro Interview Guidelines for Diagnosing the Autism Spectrum, Second Edition (MIGDAS-2)**

  a   Sensory-based interview for gathering and organising the qualitative information needed to diagnose autism in children and adults.
  b   The process includes guidelines for gathering information from parents/caregivers and teachers.

When assessing for autism it is important to consider **differential diagnosis**. [9] Common conditions which often need to be considered during an autism diagnosis include LD, ADHD, Social Communication Disorder, Anxiety, Hearing Impairment, Attachment Disorder, Tourette's, OCD, Personality Disorder, trauma, and Sensory Processing Difficulties. Very often a detailed developmental history, clinical interview, and targeted psychometric testing will help to discern whether the presentation most fits a diagnosis of autism or another condition. There are some additional tools which can help guide decision making further, for example the Coventry Grid [19] can help differentiate between complex trauma and autism.

Adaptations and considerations

✓   Make the world accessible: adjust, adapt, accommodate.
✓   The autism spectrum is not linear and as such there are a multitude of ways that autism presents. Each autistic person has strengths and needs which are context- and time dependant. Therefore, it is imperative to ensure that all support is reflective of this.

✓ Ask the person to identify reasonable adjustments that might help them, such as changes to their environment (lights, crowds, noise, etc.), schedule, or tasks.

✓ Ensure that the person is informed of upcoming events with enough time to plan for these. Where possible try to ensure events happen as planned.

✓ Provide information in advance to allow the person time to process this. If this is not possible, ensure that information is provided at a slow pace, using key words and repeating where necessary.

✓ Do not rely on non-verbal communication (facial expressions, body language, eye-contact).

✓ Use clear communication, avoid sarcasm, irony, idioms and figurative speech. Ensure that questions asked are specific and if there is a possible double meaning clarify what it is you are asking.

✓ Remember that autistic people may experience increased anxiety in social situations or as a result of unexpected change.

✓ Be aware of the potential for 'sensory overload' leading to either a meltdown[10] or shutdown[11] for the person.

✓ Autistic people can find it difficult to express their wants, needs, and emotions so consider finding suitable ways to support them with this (e.g. flashcards, social stories, modify your own verbal communication, use assistive technology).

✓ It can be difficult for an autistic person to restart a task which they have stopped (and vice versa), this is known as 'autistic inertia' and it important to account for this when interacting with autistic individuals.

✓ Stimming can provide an autistic person with predictable sensory feedback and help to regulate internal experiences.

✓ Make sure to familiarise yourself with the strengths of the autistic person as well as those areas they find challenging.

✓ Ensure you are aware of communication preferences, sensory sensitivities, and preferred routines.

✓ Increase self-awareness in relation to sensory experiences and making adaptations to the environment to suit.

The DSM-5-TR recommends three levels of support for those diagnosed with autism. It is important when speaking about these levels of support that it is recognised that support may vary depending on the area of need or even simply from day to day.

There are a number of areas of functioning for which targeted attention should be paid. These include 'the double empathy problem', cognitive flexibility, and executive functioning.

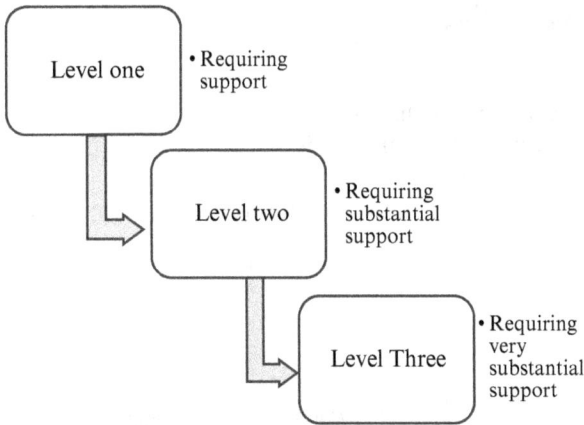

Figure 3.2 DSM-5-TR: three levels of support

Empathy is the ability to share and understand the feelings of another. Cognitive empathy is the ability to comprehend what someone else is feeling or thinking by interpreting their body language or facial expressions in line with the social context. Affective empathy is feeling the feelings of others. Autistic people can often experience high levels of affective empathy. The *double empathy problem* [20] highlights the difficulties experienced (e.g. in communication styles, expectation, perception, and values) when autistic and neurotypical people interact with each other. It is important to bear in mind that autistic people can show high levels of affective and cognitive empathy with other autistic people; however, difficulties may arise in interactions between autistic and neurotypical individuals.

Cognitive flexibility is the capacity to shift between different mental tasks or strategies and adjust responses according to changing environmental input. This can reinforce the desire for predictability and structure. Providing an environment such as this can allow an autistic person to thrive.

Executive functioning includes skills such as planning, organisation, time management, and working memory (see Chapter 6). These skills have a significant impact on an individual's ability to engage with activities of daily living. Many autistic people struggle with these skills and thus with necessary tasks of self-care.

Signposting

- https://autisticnottingham.org/
- https://www.autismeastmidlands.org.uk/
- https://www.autism.org.uk/
- https://www.nottinghamshirehealthcare.nhs.uk/neurodevelopmental-specialist-service/

Precious case example

Precious is a 37-year-old woman with a diagnosis of autism. Precious works in a call centre, her role being cold calling members of the public and asking them to complete surveys following the purchase of a new car. Precious describes how this job suits her as she is provided with a script that she must follow during her calls. She often struggles when thinking of topics of conversation spontaneously, and as such having a script helps her to feel more relaxed. She says that the hardest part of her job is her lunch breaks. A hot meal is provided by the company to staff, but she often chooses not to have this because she dislikes the textures and ingredients of some of the foods provided (e.g. lasagne, curries, chillies). She will always eat the hot meal on Fridays as this is consistently fish and chips and tastes the same every week, which she finds reassuring. She also experiences discomfort during lunch breaks, feeling unsure about where to sit, her preference being to sit alone and listen to her music. However, she has been told by her manager that she should be more social with her colleagues as some have described her as 'stand off-ish' and 'aloof'. Precious does not want anyone to think badly of her so, when she does join her colleagues for lunch, she ensures that she meets all their eyes and engages fully in discussions so that they know she is interested. She will often find this very exhausting and as a result, can find it harder to complete her calls after lunch.

Precious likes to keep to the same routine each day. She wakes up and has a breakfast of Shredded Wheat and a cup of coffee. She then walks to work, often listening to the same song on repeat for the whole 25-minute commute. After work, Precious will go for a run and when she has returned home, she can spend hours at night on her laptop reading up on her favourite TV shows. Very often when

Precious is in conversation with colleagues or friends, she will quote lines from TV shows.

Precious has a group of friends whom she loves very much. However, she has always found it difficult to be in romantic relationships. She believes this is because she enjoys her own company and likes to have the time to explore her own interests, and because she often misunderstands what is expected of her in romantic relationships.

Notes

1　The characteristic way that a person's brain processes sensory stimuli.
2　A term coined by Kassiane Asasumasu to mean neurologically divergent from typical.
3　Acknowledgement of the way in which different types of discrimination are connected to and affect each other.
4　Helpful reading: Hendrickx, S. (2015). *Women and Girls with Autism Spectrum Disorder: Understanding Life Experiences from Early Childhood to Old Age*. Jessica Kingsley Publishers.
5　BPD is a disorder of mood and how a person interacts with others.
6　The National Autistic Society (NAS) is the UK's leading charity for people affected by autism.
7　The misattribution of traits of one condition to a comorbid condition.
8　Obsessive-Compulsive Disorder (OCD) is a long-lasting disorder in which a person experiences uncontrollable and recurring thoughts (obsessions), engages in repetitive behaviours (compulsions), or both.
9　The process of differentiating between two or more conditions which share similar signs or symptoms.
10　A response to an overwhelming situation that can temporarily cause a loss of control of behaviour.
11　A retreat into themselves and away from their surroundings.

References

1. O'Nions, E., Petersen, I., Buckman, J. E., Charlton, R., Cooper, C., Corbett, A., Happe, F., Manthorpe, J., Richards, M., Saunders, R., Zanker, C., Mandy, W., & Stott, J. (2023). Autism in England: assessing underdiagnosis in a population-based cohort study of prospectively collected primary care data. *The Lancet Regional Health–Europe*, 3(29). doi:10.1016/j.lanepe.2023.100626.
2. Hill, E. L. & Frith, U. (2003). Understanding autism: Insights from mind and brain. *Philosophical Transactions of the Royal Society of London. Series B: Biological Sciences*, 358(1430), 281–289. doi:10.1098/rstb.2002.1209.
3. UK Government. (2021). The national strategy for autistic children, young people and adults 2021 to 2026. Retrieved from: https://www.gov.uk/government/publications/national-strategy-for-autistic-children-young-people-a

nd-adults-2021-to-2026/the-national-strategy-for-autistic-children-young-peo
ple-and-adults-2021-to-2026.

4. NHS England Digital. (2024). Health and care of people with learning disabilities, experimental statistics 2022 to 2023. Retrieved from: https://digital.
nhs.uk/data-and-information/publications/statistical/health-and-care-of-peop
le-with-learning-disabilities.

5. World Health Organisation. (2022). *International Classification of Diseases*
(11th Revision). World Health Organisation.

6. American Psychiatric Association. (2022). *Diagnostic and Statistical Manual
of Mental Disorders* (5th ed., text rev.) American Psychiatric Association.

7. Tromans, S., Chester, V., Gemegah, E., Roberts, K., Morgan, Z., Yao, G. L.,
& Brugha, T. (2021). Autism identification across ethnic groups: A narrative
review. *Advances in Autism*, 7(3), 241–255. doi:10.1108/AIA-03-2020-0017.

8. Adak, B. & Halder, S. (2017). Systematic review on prevalence for autism
spectrum disorder with respect to gender and socio-economic status. *Journal of
Mental Disorders and Treatment*, 3(1), 1–31. doi:10.4172/2471-271X.1000133.

9. Hull, L. & Mandy, W. (2021). Camouflaging Autistic Traits Questionnaire
(CAT-Q). F. R. Volkmar (Ed.). *Encyclopaedia of Autism Spectrum Disorders*, 795–797. Springer.

10. Roestorf, A., Bowler, D. M., Deserno, M. K., Howlin, P., Klinger, L.,
McConachie, H., Parr, J. R., Powel, P., Van Heijst, B. F. C. & Geurts, H. M.
(2019). 'Older Adults with ASD: The Consequences of Aging'. Insights from
a series of special interest group meetings held at the International Society
for Autism Research 2016–2017. *Research in Autism Spectrum Disorders*, 63
(3), 3–12. doi:10.1016/j.rasd.2018.08.00.

11. Brown, C. M., Attwood, T., Garnett M., & Stokes, M. A. (2020), 'Am I
autistic? Utility of the Girls Questionnaire for Autism Spectrum Condition as
an autism assessment in adult women. *Autism in Adulthood*, 2(3), 216–226.
doi:10.1089/aut.2019.0054.

12. Sedgewick, F., Crane, L., Hill, V., & Pellicano, E. (2019). Friends and
lovers: The relationships of autistic and neurotypical women. *Autism in
Adulthood*, 1(2), 112–123. doi:10.1089/aut.2018.0028.

13. de Leeuw, A., Happé, F., & Hoekstra, R. A. (2020). A conceptual framework for understanding the cultural and contextual factors on autism across
the globe. *Autism Research*, 13(7), 1029–1050. doi:10.1002/aur.2276.

14. Mandell, D. S., Ittenbach, R. F., Levy, S. E., & Pinto-Martin, J. A. (2007).
Disparities in diagnoses received prior to a diagnosis of autism spectrum
disorder. *Journal of Autism and Developmental Disorders, 3(*9), 1795–1802.
doi:10.1007/s10803-006-0314-8.

15. Gupta, N., & Gupta, M. (2023). Diagnostic overshadowing in high-functioning autism: Mirtazapine, buspirone, and Modified Cognitive Behavioral Therapy (CBT) as treatment options. *Cureus*, 15(5). doi:10.7759/cureus.39446.

16. Tek, S., & Landa, R. J. (2012). Differences in autism symptoms between
minority and non-minority toddlers. *Journal of Autism and Developmental
Disorders*, 42(9), 1967–1973. doi:10.1007/s10803-012-1445-8.

17. National Institute for Health and Care Excellence. (2021). NICE guidelines, autism spectrum disorder in adults: Diagnosis and management (CG142, 2021) Retrieved from: https://www.nice.org.uk/guidance/cg142.

18. NHS England (2023). A national framework to deliver improved outcomes in all-age autism assessment pathways: Guidance for integrated care boards. Retrieved from: https://www.england.nhs.uk/long-read/a-national-framework-to-deliver-improved-outcomes-in-all-age-autism-assessment-pathways-guidance-for-integrated-care-boards/.

19. Cox, C., Bulluss, E., Chapman, F., Cookson, A., Flood, A., & Sharp, A. (2019). The Coventry Grid for adults: A tool to guide clinicians in differentiating complex trauma and autism. *Good Autism Practice*, 20(1). doi:10.1108/AIA-07-2023-0041.

20. Milton, D. E. (2012). On the ontological status of autism: The 'double empathy problem'. *Disability & Society*, 27(6), 883–887. doi:10.1080/09687599.2012.710008.

4 Brain injury

Sarah Ashworth-Watts

CONSULTANT FORENSIC PSYCHOLOGIST

ⓘ Introduction

Note: Whilst not traditionally considered a neurodiverse condition, it was considered important to include acquired brain injury within this book due to the idea that people's brains function differently in a variety of ways. This can be for many different reasons including injury and/or illness.

Brain injury is the leading cause of death and disability worldwide. Of all types of injury, those to the brain are among the most likely to result in death or permanent disability. As clinicians, it is possible that we will come across individuals who have been affected by a brain injury at some point in their life, some of whom may be aware that they have suffered an injury, and others who may not.

As professionals, we may come into contact with people who have experienced an acquired brain injury as they are going through the education system, through health or social care systems, or even becoming involved with the criminal justice system. This chapter will provide an overview of the brain, its structure and function, give an explanation as to some of the common terms used, and explore some of the potential effects of a brain injury, with the aim of developing our clinical responsivity to meet the needs of this population.

It is important to remember that a brain injury can occur at any age after birth. However certain age groups are more at risk than others. Those below the age of 5 years old, those aged between 13 and 22 years old, and those over 75 years old are at increased risk of acquiring a brain injury. This is due to a variety of factors including physical differences and lifestyle choices (e.g. physical vulnerability during

DOI: 10.4324/9781003510659-4

infancy, increased chance of engaging in risk behaviours such as unsafe driving during teenage years, increased likelihood of falling in older age). The effects of a brain injury vary widely; they can be serious or mild, temporary or permanent, immediate or delayed. Generally, road traffic accidents cause around half of all brain injuries, although the leading cause of injury varies based upon individual factors such as sex, race, and age. These will all be discussed later in the chapter.

This chapter is divided into the following sections:

1 Background
2 Heterogeneity within brain injury
3 Things to look out for
4 Screening assessments
5 Specialist assessment
6 Adaptations and considerations
7 Signposting
8 Case examples
9 References

Background

The **brain** is the most complex structure in the human body. It comprises three main areas, the **cerebrum**, the **cerebellum**, and the **brain stem**.

- The **cerebrum** is the largest part of the brain. It is made up of grey matter (the **cerebral cortex**) on the outside, and white matter in the centre. The cerebrum is divided into the left and right **hemispheres**, connected in the centre by a large white matter tract called the **corpus callosum**. The cerebrum contains four lobes:

  a The **frontal lobe** is the largest area of the cerebrum and is situated at the front of the head behind the forehead. It is involved with our actions and decision making, our emotions, judgments, our ability to plan and problem solve, our levels of intelligence, concentration, and self-awareness.

  b The **parietal lobe**, located behind the frontal lobes towards the crown of the head, interprets signals from vision, hearing, motor, sensory and memory. It is involved with our spatial awareness, and our sense of touch, pain, and temperature. It helps us understand and interact with the outside world.

  c The **temporal lobe** is the second largest area of the cerebrum and is situated on the side of the brain, behind the temples.

This area is involved with understanding language, memory, hearing, sequencing, and organisation.

d   The **occipital lobe**, situated at the back of the head, receives information from our eyes, and interprets what we see (e.g. colour, light, movement).

• The **cerebellum** is at the back under the cerebrum. It is involved with coordinating muscle movements, keeping posture, and balance.

• The **brainstem** connects the brain to the spinal cord. It controls our automatic functions such as breathing, heart rate, body temperature, wake and sleep cycles, digestion, sneezing, coughing, vomiting, and swallowing.

> **Note:** It can be helpful to imagine the 'hand' model of the brain. Think of your arm as the spinal cord, and at the top your wrist as the brain stem and the heel of your hand as the cerebellum (the lower brain, responsible for basic survival). Your thumb, tucked into your palm, represents the limbic system (the midbrain, the embedded 'animal' part responsible for emotional reactions. Your fingers, wrapped around your thumb, act as the cerebrum (the upper brain, responsible for more complex processes).

It is helpful to know what **processes** each region is involved with, as damage to that area can affect the functioning of these processes. However, it is important to remember that the brain is complex, with many different connections between the various areas. As such, whilst damage to a specific part of the brain may affect the tasks that are typically associated with that area, wider functioning may also be affected. Therefore, the picture of brain injury is very rarely simple and often has widespread implications for an individual's life.

A **head injury** is an umbrella term which refers to any sort of injury to your head which can affect your brain, skull, or scalp. This can range from a mild bump or bruise to a more serious injury to the brain. Even after a seemingly minor head injury, the brain's function can be affected, and this is sometimes referred to as **concussion**. Concussion can cause difficulties such as headaches, dizziness, fatigue, depression, irritability, and memory issues. Clinically we may see increased rates of concussions within contact sports, such as boxing, or sports where there are repeated blows to the head such as rugby or football where someone is training to head the ball.

An **acquired brain injury** is an injury caused to the brain, which occurs after birth. In general, brain injuries can be split into two groups based on their causation: traumatic and non-traumatic injuries. It is important that we as clinicians remember that the term trauma is used within this context to refer to an external force, rather than reflecting a psychological trauma.

- **Traumatic injuries** are caused by an external force (trauma) usually to the head, damaging the brain. A trauma in this context is a sudden, external, physical assault. A TBI can be **open**, where the skull is broken or penetrated in some way (e.g. a gunshot wound), or **closed**, where the skull remains intact (e.g. a blow with an object).
- **Non-traumatic** injuries are damage caused to the brain due to conditions, illnesses, or infections. Examples include neurodegenerative conditions (e.g. Huntington's, Alzheimer's, Parkinson's, motor neurone disease); organic conditions (e.g. brain tumours, strokes, encephalitis, epilepsy, hydrocephalus, haemorrhages, meningitis); toxins (e.g. alcohol or substance related conditions, petrol and glue inhalation, industrial neurotoxins); and hypoxia/anoxia which is reduced oxygen flow to the brain (e.g. ligation, drowning, overdose, cardiac arrest, suffocating).

When talking about brain injury **onset**, there are various terms used to differentiate between the impact an event has upon the brain structure (which refers to how the parts of the brain are arranged or formed physically) and function (which refers to how the brain works). The brain is suspended within the skull by a clear fluid called **cerebrospinal fluid** (CSF). This acts as a shock absorber and helps ensure an even pressure within the brain. If the head is hit, the brain may move around, hitting the sides of the skull. A **coup** injury refers to the damage at the site that has been hit. A **contrecoup** injury refers to the damage to the opposite side of the injury site, as the brain moves. The inside of the skull also has bony **ridges** which form when the pieces of the skull fuse together. If the brain comes into contact with these ridges, it can cause damage to various areas of the brain.

The term **primary brain injury** refers to the impact on the brain at the time of the injury (e.g. damage to the area at the impact site). **Secondary brain injury** refers to the changes that can happen in the hours to days after the first injury (e.g. bleeding and swelling on the brain which can cause further damage to other areas). This damage can be **focal** (in one place) or **diffuse** (all over).

A relatively common example of a diffuse injury is **diffuse axonal injury** which can be caused by a quick movement or fast stopping of the head. This can cause the brain to move around, causing bundles of **nerve fibres** in the brain to be stretched, torn, or **sheared**. Examples include shaking injuries, whiplash type injuries, fast deceleration injuries (e.g. road traffic accidents, which are one of the most common causes of ABI).

In serious cases, a brain injury can cause problems with consciousness, awareness, alertness, and responsiveness. There are four abnormal states that can result from a severe brain injury:

- Those individuals with severely altered **consciousness** who still display some evidence of self-awareness or awareness of their environment (e.g. are able to follow simple commands or provide a yes/no response) are referred to as being in a **minimally conscious state**.
- A **vegetative state** can occur as a result of extensive damage to the brain. Those in a vegetative state are unconscious and unaware of their surroundings; however, there can be periods of unresponsive alertness (where they may groan, move, or show reflex responses). If someone is in this state for longer than a few weeks, it is known as a **persistent vegetative state**.
- A person in a **coma** is unconscious, unaware, and unable to respond to external stimuli such as pain or light. Coma generally lasts a few days or weeks, after which the person may regain consciousness, die, or move into a vegetative state.
- The term **brain death** refers to a lack of measurable brain function and activity after an extended period. This is usually confirmed by investigations which indicate no blood flow to the brain.

It is important to seek **medical attention** immediately if you suspect someone is suffering from the acute effects of a brain injury. However, it is possible that as clinicians we will encounter people who have been living with the consequences of a brain injury for some time, sometimes without awareness. Brain injuries can impact upon all aspects of functioning including physical effects, behavioural changes, cognitive difficulties, and emotional differences. Therefore, clinicians need to be aware of, and alert to, the potential effects so we are able to respond effectively to the individual's needs. These can have a significant impact upon the individual's functioning and upon the lives of their loved ones.

Alongside the direct effects of a brain injury, we must also consider the **psychological impact** that the circumstances associated with the injury may have had for the person (e.g. post-traumatic stress disorder following a road traffic accident; depression following a diagnosis of a degenerative disorder such as Huntington's Disease; anxiety regarding a critical ongoing health condition such as a brain tumour), and how the individual has **adjusted** to, or attempted to manage, any changes following onset (e.g. denial, relationship changes, substance misuse). The wider response of their social support systems will also be important, for example the adaptations from their friends and family members, or the reaction of their work colleagues and neighbours.

Heterogeneity within brain injury

Whilst brain injury can affect anyone, at any point in their life, there are certain individuals who are at increased risk of acquiring a brain injury. Certain groups are more vulnerable than others, owing to interactions between biological, behavioural, social, and cultural factors. Furthermore, these factors may also influence the consequences of such injury, shaping the individual's response, biologically and psychologically.

The pathway from injury onset to disability is affected by a multitude of factors, from the micro to the macro, including biological differences, attitudes at local, familial, and societal levels, socioeconomic factors, and legislative considerations. Consideration of the interrelated factors involved will hopefully support clinicians to develop a better understanding of the different mechanisms that shape the health status trajectory and outcomes of an acquired brain injury.

The examples of age, sex and gender, socioeconomic status, and race and ethnicity are given here for clinicians to consider within their practice. However, these examples are by no means exhaustive.

Age

The brain develops throughout the lifespan, particularly during childhood, with different areas developing at different rates. Experiencing a brain injury during key **critical periods** of brain development can affect the normal formation of brain networks. Furthermore, if the injury is sustained or has onset before a certain area has fully developed, it may be that the effects do not become apparent until the individual matures, and particularly as they reach different developmental stages ('growing into deficit'). It may be that the effects of a brain injury are not immediately obvious, particularly in the case of brain injury sustained during childhood (**paediatric brain injury**). For example, the effects of a brain injury sustained at an early age may not become apparent until the child reaches adolescence and is required to manage multiple complex relationship dynamics. This is markedly relevant with the **executive functioning** skills, which are some of the last to become fully developed.

Children with brain injury may have difficulty developing new cognitive skills. This can impact upon learning ability more generally, and so whilst the injury may not have directly impacted upon a specific skill, the process of skill acquisition, retention and refinement may be affected. As such, the effects of an injury may become more generalised over time. Psychosocial problems such as depression, anxiety, social difficulties, aggression, and sleep disturbances may also become more apparent as they mature, and different expectations are placed upon them.

Following injury, the brain can, however, respond to damage by creating new neural networks to take over functions that were previously managed by the damaged area. This is referred to as **neuroplasticity**. These adaptations can take place both on a structural and functional level. Neuroplasticity is thought to be superior in childhood and adolescence (when the brain is still developing) than it would be if the injury occurred during adulthood. However, if reorganisation of function does occur, it may lead to a **crowding effect.** Crowding can be seen as the 'price to pay' for neuroplasticity, in which multiple functions are subsumed by less brain, which may result in a depression of general abilities. Nevertheless, it is important to remember that neuroplasticity is not unlimited, and that it is affected by many factors such as an individual's genetics, lifestyle, and environment.

Sex and gender

The effects of biological sex, as well as gender, represent a constellation of biological, behavioural, social, and cultural elements that can impact the nature and course of brain injury. For the purposes of this section, the term sex refers to the physical and biological aspects of an individual, which make someone biologically male or female. The term gender refers to the socially constructed roles, expectations, and behaviours that are often ascribed to the different sexes.

Initially, it should be recognised that there is an issue of **sex-based bias** in neuroscience research generally, where within animal research male rodents have predominantly been used as an experimental injury model, and in human research fewer women than men are recruited to clinical trials [1]. This has implications for the generalisations we are able to make from experimentally based conclusions [2].

There are differences in the way men and women are likely to acquire brain injuries, with women being more likely to acquire injuries through assault and intimate partner violence and men through falls and road traffic accidents [3]. This may have implications for the types of injuries men and women are likely to sustain (e.g. site of damage).

In addition, there are sex-specific differences in post-injury complications which may in part be due to sex-based genetics and sex hormones which influence relevant biological responses to injury, such as **inflammation, oedema**, and **mitochondrial function**. For example, female steroid hormones exert **neuroprotective** effects through the anti-inflammatory and antioxidant mechanisms [4]. Sex-based differences also impact **neuroplasticity**, meaning that the process of recovery may be different in biological men and women [5], with women showing a greater potential for plasticity and reorganisation.

Finally, there can be **gender disparities** in norms and role expectations placed upon males and females, which may affect the reported prevalence and incidence of brain injury. For example, it may be more socially acceptable for a woman who has sustained a brain injury to leave employment and be supported financially by her husband, or a man who sustains a sporting injury may be less likely to seek medical attention than a woman due to a fear of appearing less masculine.

Socioeconomic status

Following brain injury, one of the key factors which researchers have found to play a central role throughout the recovery process is that of socioeconomic differences [6].

Within the field of brain injury rehabilitation, lower social economic status has been found to be associated with higher rates of depression and anxiety, reduced life satisfaction, poorer community integration, limited access to appropriate outpatient care, reduced neurocognitive performance, and alarmingly, higher mortality rates [7]. These differences become more pronounced the more severe the brain injury is. There may be many variables involved with this process, such as levels of social deprivation, degree of **cognitive reserve** (the brain's natural resistance to injury), accessibility of adequate health care, and access to care resources.

Race and ethnicity

The impact of race and ethnicity on brain injury is a complex area of study. There are racial disparities in terms of who is at greater risk of acquiring a brain injury and via what route these may be sustained. For example, research in America has demonstrated that certain ethnic minorities such as black African Americans are at greater risk of suffering TBIs from violence as compared to non-Hispanic white Americans [8].

Studies have highlighted the numerous ways in which racial and ethnic disparities span the continuum of care, including acute care and diagnosis, post-TBI recovery and adjustment, and long-term outcomes [9]. Certain racial and ethnic minorities (for example non-Hispanic Black and Hispanic individuals) are at increased risk of poor outcomes following a TBI [10]. Outcomes included longer hospital stays, medical complications, increased mortality rates, higher inpatient costs, and worse hospital disposition.

Further to this, the differences in caregiver roles and burden based on race and ethnicity is also a relevant topic. Differences in reported levels of caregiver burden, levels of distress experienced, types of coping strategies employed, and caregiver ideologies have been found between various racial and ethnic groups [11]. However, it should be remembered that results are varied, and further research is recommended. Nevertheless, differences in approaches and coping strategies in caregiving roles should be considered when working clinically with individuals and their support systems.

In summary, this section has aimed to highlight the degree of diversity within the field of brain injury, whether that be in relation to certain groups' vulnerability to sustaining a brain injury, physiological responses to a brain injury, rehabilitation outcomes, or even the reaction and response of family and friends. This section has introduced some of the relevant issues; however, it is intended as an overview, a reflective point for clinical consideration, and a starting point for further reading.

(⚑) Things to look out for

It is not always possible to tell through observation alone that an individual has sustained a brain injury. They may have obvious signs of injury or illness (e.g. a visible scar, skull depression), but many brain injuries are **non-visible**. This has led to brain injury being considered as a **'hidden disability'** in many cases, which can result in a lack of appropriate understanding and support being offered.

Whilst we may not be able to 'see' the brain injury, we may be able to see some of the changes that have manifested for the individual following the onset. This can be a real challenge for clinicians as we may not have a clear picture of what an individual's abilities, personality and general presentation was like prior to the injury. It is crucial to discuss any changes they, family members or friends may have noticed since the onset of illness or injury.

Q	**Physical** indicators may include difficulty moving around, an unusual gait (shuffling, hesitant, wide stance), poor balance, falling, increased rigidity of muscles (**spasticity**), weakness or paralysis, loss of coordination of voluntary muscle movements (**ataxia**), fatigue (e.g. spending more time in bed), choking or difficulty swallowing (**dysphagia**), difficulty with speech (**dysarthria**), reports of headaches, dizziness, and sensory impairment.
Q	**Behavioural** changes can include increased irritability, aggression, sexual behaviours, impulsiveness, disinhibition, seemingly obsessive behaviours, repetitive actions (**perseveration**), lack of activity due to low motivation and initiative (**apathy**), difficulties with relationships (e.g. arguments, relationship breakdown).
Q	**Cognitive** symptoms could include confusion, disorientation, forgetfulness, rigid thinking, difficulty understanding, reduced processing speed, poor planning, concentration difficulties, generating false memories without the intention to deceive (**confabulation**), repetition in conversation, impaired insight and empathy, difficulty understanding others' points of view (**egocentricity**), difficulty making decisions, and apparent changes to what some can see and/or perceive (**visual-perceptual impairment**).
Q	**Emotional** signs might include instability, lability, mood swings, shorter temper, flattened affect, lack of interest, depression and sense of loss, reduced self-esteem, anxiety, frustration and anger, and personality changes.

Figure 4.1 Things to look out for

Screening assessments

In the first instance, it is important to gather information about the person's history to see whether there is any evidence of events, situations or circumstances which may have caused a brain injury. This could include asking about their developmental history, obtaining a medical history including family history, and completing a clinical interview exploring significant life events.

It is important that an accurate and detailed clinical history is gained, in addition to information about their lifestyle, activities, hobbies or interests, as sports such as rugby or boxing are associated with increased risk of sustaining a head injury, and certain lifestyle choices such as substance or alcohol misuse may increase an individual's risk, or vulnerability.

Asking the person questions such as: whether they have ever been diagnosed with a neurological condition likely to affect their brain (e.g. meningitis); have they ever sustained a brain injury; ever lost consciousness, felt dizzy or vomited following a blow to the head, or noticed any changes to their functioning (e.g. *'have you noticed any recent difficulties with your memory?', 'has anyone mentioned that you've changed since the accident?', 'do you every have problems finding the right words for things?', 'are you experiencing any new headaches?').*

If they report any changes, explore the nature of the onset of these differences. Was this **acute** in nature (e.g. sudden and marked) or subtle over time? Were they associated with any event (e.g. an accident or illness)? Are the difficulties made worse by anything (e.g. if they have not had enough sleep) or do they notice any particular fluctuations?

There are specific tools which can be used to find out if someone has a higher chance of having a brain injury. These include tools to structure a clinical interview, questionnaires (which ask whether people have been in situations where they were likely to sustain a brain injury, whether they are part of a high-risk group, or have experienced symptoms associated with a brain injury), and screening assessments which evaluate cognitive functioning across various domains, which may indicate impaired or atypical levels of functioning.

It is important to remember that none of these instruments are diagnostic and should always be interpreted by a clinician in conjunction with other factors, including a clinical history, risk factors, and medical investigations. Additionally, there are some stipulations regarding the access and qualification level required to use some of the suggested instruments, so it is important to ensure that clinicians are familiar with these prior to utilising any of the following tools.

- The **Brain Injury Screening Tool (BIST)** [12] is designed to support the clinical interview process for those thought that have sustained a brain injury. It helps the clinician gather information about how the injury was sustained, loss of consciousness, and presence of possible risk factors, in addition to exploring the level of risk of acute and chronic problems associated with a brain injury.
- The **Brain Injury Screening Index (BISI)** [13] is a validated screening tool which helps practitioners gather an individual's self-reported history of brain injury. It can be used within prison, probation, community, and rehabilitation settings to establish whether someone has sustained a brain injury.
- The **Montreal Cognitive Assessment (MoCA)** [14] is a validated cognitive screening instrument for the early detection of mild cognitive impairment. It evaluates several cognitive domains (executive functions, language, orientation, calculations, conceptual thinking, memory, visual perception, attention and concentration) and is

particularly useful for detecting cognitive changes in those with higher levels of education.

- The **Mini-Mental Status Exam (MMSE)** [15] is a cognitive screening tool to identify cognitive impairment, to estimate the severity of the impairment, and to document cognitive change over time. It tests six cognitive domains (orientation, repetition, verbal recall, attention and calculation, language, and visual construction).
- The **Oxford Cognitive Screen (OCS)** [16] is a stroke-specific cognitive screening tool. It is designed to be administered with, and identify, domain-specific post-stroke cognitive problems (e.g., apraxia, neglect, aphasia, reading and writing impairments). It covers five cognitive domains (language, attention, memory, praxis, number).
- The **Repeatable Battery for the Assessment of Neuropsychological Status Update (RBANS Update)** [17] is a brief, individually administered battery used to assess neuropsychological status. It assesses five cognitive domains (immediate memory, visuospatial/constructional, language, attention, delayed memory).

Specialist assessment

A **neurological examination** will consider motor and sensory skills, test hearing and speech, coordination and balance, mental status, and changes in mood or behaviour. The **Glasgow Coma Scale** [18] is the most widely used tool for assessing the level of consciousness a person has after a potential brain injury. The standardised test measures the person's ability to open their eyes (eye), respond to verbal prompts (verbal response), and respond by moving their body (motor response).

When necessary, medical professionals will use **brain imaging technology** to evaluate the extent of the brain injury and help decide whether surgical intervention is required to help repair any damage or minimise negative consequences to the brain (e.g. swelling). This depends upon the medical examination and the symptoms present. Common scans include **computed tomography (CT)** which is the recommended scan to assess people with suspected moderate to severe brain injury, and **magnetic resonance imaging (MRI)** which produces detailed images of body tissue, which is recommended for use after the acute phase, due to this being a more sensitive test that is able to pick up subtle changes that the CT scan may be unable to detect. **Functional MRI (fMRI)** measures brain activity by detecting changes associated with blood flow; these scans can be used to understand how a brain injury has affected the way the brain functions.

Neuropsychological tests to examine brain functioning are often used along with imaging in people who have suffered mild brain injury. Such tests involve performing specific cognitive tasks. Some examples of commonly used tests are provided in Figure 4.2.

There are some additional considerations to keep in mind when thinking about someone's performance on neuropsychological assessments:

It is important to think about the **physical state** of the person being assessed; pain or discomfort may impact upon concentration, as can **fatigue, hunger,** or **thirst.** Some **infections** are known to effect cognitive functioning (e.g. urinary tract infections can have a significant impact on cognition), as can some **medications** (e.g. anticholinergic drugs can cause memory problems), or whether someone has consumed **alcohol** or **illicit substances,** which can impact on performance for days, weeks, maybe months after use.

Some **emotional or psychological states** can impact upon an individual's functioning. For example, **depression** can impact on motivation, attention, concentration and can slow responses. A little **anxiety** can improve performance; however, too much is likely to impair it. An individual suffering from symptoms relating to **post traumatic stress disorder** may have altered attention or memory. Where an individual is experiencing **psychosis**, it is possible that the associated symptomatology may overshadow other conditions or impair their executive functioning. And finally, an individual experiencing **apathy** may find that their motivation is impaired.

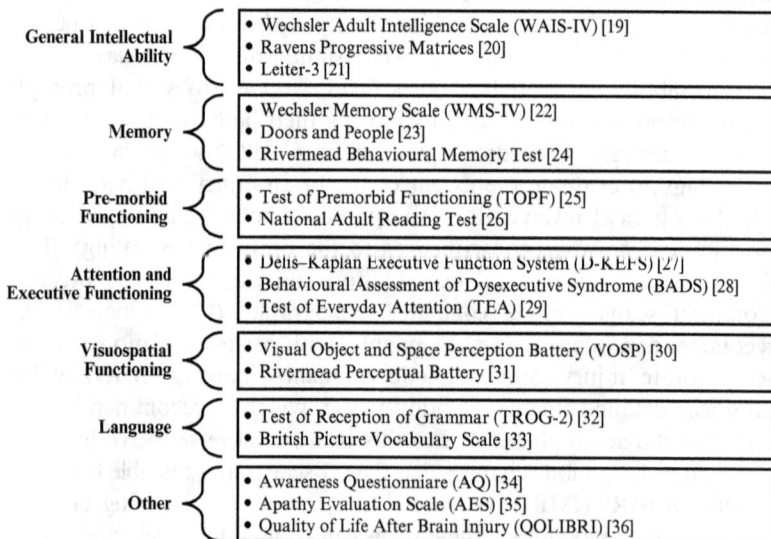

General Intellectual Ability	• Wechsler Adult Intelligence Scale (WAIS-IV) [19] • Ravens Progressive Matrices [20] • Leiter-3 [21]
Memory	• Wechsler Memory Scale (WMS-IV) [22] • Doors and People [23] • Rivermead Behavioural Memory Test [24]
Pre-morbid Functioning	• Test of Premorbid Functioning (TOPF) [25] • National Adult Reading Test [26]
Attention and Executive Functioning	• Delis–Kaplan Executive Function System (D-KEFS) [27] • Behavioural Assessment of Dysexecutive Syndrome (BADS) [28] • Test of Everyday Attention (TEA) [29]
Visuospatial Functioning	• Visual Object and Space Perception Battery (VOSP) [30] • Rivermead Perceptual Battery [31]
Language	• Test of Reception of Grammar (TROG-2) [32] • British Picture Vocabulary Scale [33]
Other	• Awareness Questionniare (AQ) [34] • Apathy Evaluation Scale (AES) [35] • Quality of Life After Brain Injury (QOLIBRI) [36]

Figure 4.2 Commonly used neuropsychological tests

As such, it can be useful to get an understanding of some of these factors within the context of neuropsychological assessment. **Standard tools** may be useful (such as the Becks Depression or Anxiety Inventories) or **adapted** tools may be more appropriate to meet the needs of the individual (such as the Glasgow Depression [37] and Anxiety [38] Scales – Learning Disability).

Furthermore, **effort** tests should be completed routinely as part of a comprehensive assessment (British Psychological Society recommendations) including clinical observation and comment. There are some specialised assessments of effort, and embedded measures of effort within certain tests. However, details should not be shared to protect test security.

Adaptations and considerations

✓ **Ask** the individual if they have ever experienced a head injury. If so, enquire whether they lost consciousness and for how long; did they notice any changes in the short term (e.g. dizziness, vomiting) or long term (e.g. significant changes to things they were previously able to do or changes to their level of functioning)?

✓ Providing information and **psychoeducation** about the potential effects of brain injury can help people better understand themselves and their current experiences (see Signposting section below for useful resources).

✓ If the individual agrees, information can be **shared** with their family members so they can also develop their understanding of their loved one's situation and provide appropriate support.

✓ Think about your **style**; be patient, flexible, and supportive.

✓ Explain things in clear, calm, simple language.

✓ If someone is struggling to understand, do not **overload** them with information but pick out the key pieces and focus on those.

✓ Be prepared to repeat information or provide a summary of what has been discussed for them to take away and refer to.

✓ Consider getting input from a **Speech and Language Therapist**. They may be able to provide support regarding communication skills, or any difficulties with swallowing, eating or drinking.

✓ Focus on short-term goals and break down tasks into smaller steps that are easier to achieve (e.g. those that might be likely to provide **intrinsic reinforcement**).

✓ Allow extra time to **process** information, to digest any instructions and then to use that information to make decisions.

✓   Consider offering regular brain **breaks**. Some people with a brain injury may struggle to concentrate after 20/30 minutes, so use short 5-minute breaks.

✓   Support the use of cognitive or behavioural techniques designed to overcome cognitive difficulties (**compensatory strategies**). For example, using internal mnemonic techniques to aid with memory, or the "Goal–Plan–Do–Check" strategy for help with attention difficulties [15].

✓   Try to use **errorless learning** principles (an instructional approach that minimises the opportunity for learners to make mistakes during the learning process). It is based on implicit learning, which is often less impaired than explicit learning in those with brain injury.

✓   Encourage the use of **external aids** when you notice cognitive difficulties (e.g. visual aids such as pictures may help when verbal skills are affected, memory aids such as diaries may help when memory is impaired).

Signposting

Often people who acquire a brain injury and their families know very little about this area. Following a brain injury, people's lives can be transformed. It can be helpful to signpost people to where to get support from, refer to other agencies, and provide resources for further research. It can be a daunting task but there are communities out there for people to share experiences, provide peer support and psychoeducation.

It is important to remember that brain injury affects whole families, not just individuals. The individual who has sustained a brain injury may have family members, friends, and loved ones whose lives can be dramatically impacted by the onset. The social environment of the individual is an increasingly recognised area of importance, and there are specialist support services available for family members.

↳   The **Brain Charity** – a charity that provides practical help, emotional support and social activities for people with various neurological conditions: https://www.thebraincharity.org.uk/

↳   **Headway** – a UK based charity offering support for individuals affected by brain injury: https://www.headway.org.uk/

↳   **Brainkind** offers a range of services and resources to help people with brain injury across the UK, from assessment and rehab to community support: https://brainkind.org/

Kabir case examples

Kabir was a 40-year-old man who had received a custodial sentence for the offences of stalking and harassing his ex-partner following their separation several years ago. He did well in prison, the structure and routine appeared to work well for him, and he was released into the community at his earliest release eligibility date.

However, he was quickly recalled for breaching his licence conditions by returning to the area in which he used to live (which he was prevented from returning to as this was where the victim lived) and failing to attend his appointments with Probation.

An independent psychologist was asked to complete an assessment of his cognitive functioning, and risk levels, to make recommendations about how the prison may be able to adapt standard interventions to meet his needs.

When interviewing Kabir, he reported that he had been involved in several fights with people in the community and also whilst in prison. One of these he recalled had involved him being punched in the head, falling to the ground and hitting his head on the pavement, resulting in him losing consciousness and being taken to hospital. However, he self-discharged soon as he was physically able to do so and did not attend any follow up appointments. Screening for potential brain injury demonstrated that further exploration was indicated.

Upon exploration, Kabir described how he felt that he experienced difficulties with his memory after the accident, and found it hard to manage his mood, getting angry quickly, which resulted in the breakdown of his relationship at the time. He described not being able to remember and accept that the relationship was over, and so kept going back to her in the hope that things could 'get back to normal'.

Assessment of his cognitive functioning and estimation of his premorbid functioning indicated that whilst his verbal abilities and perceptual reasoning skills remained relatively intact, there had been a significant deterioration in his processing speed and working memory, which were significantly impaired.

When asked about the circumstances which led to his recall, he stated that he could not remember his appointments, often became overwhelmed in his new accommodation, and wished to return to a familiar place, forgetting that his licence conditions prohibited him from being in that area.

As such, Kabir was provided psychoeducation to understand his injury and how this impacted him, and was signposted to several brain injury services for support. Furthermore, a formulation taking into consideration his brain injury and cognitive profile was presented so that those involved in the case could understand some of the difficulties he experienced and the context behind them. It was recommended that Kabir be supported to develop the skills to manage his emotions in a way that was accessible for him. Finally, recommendations were made to his community offender manager that upon release, appointment reminders were sent to Kabir on his mobile phone, along with regular reviews of his licence conditions.

Árdghal case examples

Árdghal was 9 years old when she returned from school one day complaining of headaches and a fever. She rested in bed, and when her mother attempted to wake her for her evening meal, she was unresponsive. She was rushed to hospital where she was diagnosed with bacterial meningitis, which involved life threatening inflammation of the meninges.[1] She received medical attention, regained consciousness and was ultimately discharged from hospital several weeks later.

Árdghal appeared to get back into the things she enjoyed without much change. She returned home, went back to school, and continued with her extracurricular activities, which involved horse riding, and spending time with her family and friends with no obvious signs that anything was different. She did report more frequent headaches from time to time, but nothing which significantly impacted upon her functioning.

Whilst at primary school, teachers who were familiar with Árdghal noted that she tended to take longer than she used to when responding to questions or instructions. From their experience of her before her illness, they knew her to be a capable child, and so they gave her extra time. However, when she progressed to secondary school, teachers noticed that she appeared to be struggling academically. Class sizes were much bigger, and the teachers did not have in depth knowledge of her presentation before her illness, and as such did not necessarily give her the same adaptations or allowances, and she felt left behind.

Whereas Árdghal had been placed in the top sets at primary school, the examinations her secondary school used to place her in classes indicated that she was well below average and was even placed in some of the bottom sets (including for Maths and English). She was upset by this, as she had always been told she was a bright, clever girl, and she was separated from most of the friends she had made at primary school.

As she got older, Árdghal began to demonstrate significant mood swings, whereby she would become irritable and angry often with no apparent reason. As increased social demands were placed upon her, Árdghal appeared to struggle even more. When attending sleepovers at her friends' houses, she would become emotional, falling out and arguing with her friends. She would become isolative, withdrawn, and would frequently contact her mother and ask her to come and collect her. This caused more problems with her friendship groups, with her peers choosing not to invite her to events and parties due to her reactions.

Árdghal's mother initially attributed this change to her becoming a teenager, but she noted that the severity of Árdghal's mood swings seemed to be at a much more intense level than her older sisters showed at a similar age. When at home Árdghal argued frequently with her sisters, and would often storm away and lock herself in her room or leave the house to go and ride her horse.

Árdghal left school at aged 16 years old and went to college to complete an apprenticeship in equine studies. She enjoyed the practical nature of the course, and it combined her passion for horse riding with her desire to pursue a career in equine therapy and rehabilitation.

Note

1 The meninges are the three membranes that surround the brain and spinal cord.

References

1. Gupte, R., Brooks, W., Vukas, R., Pierce, J. & Harris, J. (2019). Sex differences in traumatic brain injury: What we know and what we should know. *J Neurotrauma* 36(22): 3063–3091. doi:10.1089/neu.2018.6171.
2. Valera, E. M., Joseph, A. C., Snedaker, K., Breiding, M. J., Robertson, C. L., Colantonio, A., Levin, H., Pugh, M. J., Yurgelun-Todd, D., Mannix, R., Bazarian, J. J., Turtzo, L. C., Turkstra L. S., Begg, L., Cummings, D. M., & Bellgowan, P. S. F. (2021). Understanding traumatic brain injury in females: A state-of-the-art summary and future directions. *J Head Trauma Rehabil.* 36(1): E1–E17. doi:10.1097/htr.0000000000000652.

3. Colantonio, A. (2016). Sex, gender, and traumatic brain injury: A commentary. *Arch. Physical Med. Rehabil.* 97, S1–S4. doi:10.1016/j.apmr.2015.12.002.
4. Ma, C., Wu, X., Shen, X., Yang, Y., Chen, Z., Sun, X. & Wang, Z. (2019). Sex differences in traumatic brain injury: A multi-dimensional exploration in genes, hormones, cells, individuals, and society. *Chin Neurosurg J.* 5(24). doi:10.1186/s41016–41019–0173–0178.
5. Hyer, M. M., Phillips, L. L., & Neigh, G. N. (2018). Sex differences in synaptic plasticity: Hormones and beyond. *Front. Mol. Neurosci.* 11, 266. doi:10.3389/fnmol.2018.00266.
6. Haines, K. L., Nguyen, B. P., Vatsaas, C., Alger, A., Brooks, K., & Agarwal, S. K. (2019). Socioeconomic status affects outcomes after severity-stratified traumatic brain injury. *J Surg Res.* 235: 131–140. doi:10.1016/j.jss.2018.09.072.
7. Johnson, L. W. & Diaz, I. (2023). Exploring the social determinants of health and health disparities in traumatic brain injury: A scoping review. *Brain Sci.* 13(5): 707. doi:10.3390/brainsci13050707.
8. Maldonado, J., Huang, J. H., Childs, E. W., &Tharakan, B. (2023). Racial/ethnic differences in traumatic brain injury: Pathophysiology, outcomes, and future directions. *J Neurotrauma* 40(5–6): 502–513. doi:10.1089/neu.2021.0455.
9. Saadi, A., Bannon, S., Watson, E.*et al.* (2022). Racial and ethnic disparities associated with traumatic brain injury across the continuum of care: A narrative review and directions for future research. *J. Racial and Ethnic Health Disparities* 9, 786–799. doi:10.1007/s40615-021-01017-4.
10. Kelly, K. A., Patel, P. D., Salwi, S., Lovvorn, H. N. III, & Naftel, R. (2022). Socioeconomic health disparities in pediatric traumatic brain injury on a national level. *Journal of Neurosurgery: Pediatrics* 29(3): 335–341. doi:10.3171/2021.7.PEDS20820.
11. Sodders, M. D., Killien, E. Y., Stansbury, L. G., Vavilala, M. S., & Moore, M. (2020). Race/ethnicity and informal caregiver burden after traumatic brain injury: A scoping study. *Health Equity* 4(1): 304–315. doi:10.1089/heq.2020.0007.
12. Theadom, A., Hardaker, N., Bray, C., Siegert, R., Henshall, K., Forch, K., Fernando, K., King, D., Fulcher, M., Jewell, S., Shaikh, N., Gottgtroy, R. B. & Hume, P. (2021). Brain injury screening tool (BIST): Tool development, factor structure and validity. *PLoS One* 16(2). doi:10.1371/journal.pone.0246512.
13. Ramos, S. D. S., Liddement, J., Addicott, C., Fortescue, D., & Oddy, M. (2020). The development of the Brain Injury Screening Index (BISI): A self-report measure. *Neuropsychological Rehabilitation* 30(5): 948–960. doi:10.1080/09602011.2018.1526692.
14. Nasreddine, Z. S., Phillips, N. A., Bédirian V., Charbonneau, S., Whitehead, V., Collin, I., Cummings, J. L., & Chertkow, H. (2005). The Montreal Cognitive Assessment, MoCA: A brief screening tool for mild cognitive impairment. *Journal of the American Geriatric Society* 53(4): 695–699. doi:10.1111/j.1532-5415.2005.53221.x.

15. Folstein, M. F., Folstein, S. E., & McHugh, P. R. (1975). Mini-Mental State Examination (MMS, MMSE): A practical method for grading the cognitive state of patients for the clinician. *Journal of Psychiatric Res.* 12(3): 189–198. doi:10.1016/0022-3956(75)90026-90026.
16. Demeyere, N., Riddoch, M. J., Slavkova, E. D., Bickerton, W-L., & Humphreys, G. W. (2015). The Oxford Cognitive Screen (OCS): Validation of a stroke-specific short cognitive screening tool. *Psychological Assessment* 27 (3): 883–894. doi:10.1037/pas0000082.
17. Randolph, C. (2009). *RBANS Update: Repeatable Battery for the Assessment of Neuropsychological Status: Manual.* Bloomington, MN: Pearson.
18. Jain, S. & Iverson L. M. (2023). Glasgow Coma Scale. *StatPearls* [Internet]. Treasure Island FL: StatPearls Publishing.
19. Wechsler, D. (2008). *Wechsler Adult Intelligence Scale. Fourth Edition.* UK: Pearson Clinical Assessments.
20. Raven, J. & Raven, J. (2003). Raven Progressive Matrices. In R. S. McCallum (Ed.), *Handbook of Nonverbal Assessment* (pp. 223–237). Springer.
21. Roid, G. H. & Koch, C. (2017). Leiter-3: Nonverbal Cognitive and Neuropsychological Assessment. In McCallum, R. (Ed.), *Handbook of Nonverbal Assessment.* Cham: Springer.
22. Wechsler, D. (2009). *Advanced Clinical Solutions for WAIS-IV and WMS-IV.* San Antonio TX: Pearson.
23. Morris, R. G., Abrahams, S., Baddeley, A. D., & Polkey, C. E. (1995). Doors and people: Visual and verbal memory after unilateral temporal lobectomy. *Neuropsychology* 9(4): 464–469. doi:10.1037/0894-4105.9.4.464.
24. Kurtz, M. M. (2011). Rivermead Behavioral Memory Test. In Kreutzer, J. S., DeLuca, J., & Caplan, B. (Eds) *Encyclopedia of Clinical Neuropsychology.* New York: Springer.
25. Wechsler, D. (2011). *Test of Premorbid Functioning – UK Version.* London: Pearson Clinical Assessments.
26. Nelson, H. E. & Willison, J. (1991). *National Adult Reading Test (NART).* Windsor: Nfer-Nelson.
27. Delis, D. C., Kaplan E., & Kramer, J. H. (2001). *Delis Kaplan Executive Function System (D-KEFS).* San Antonio TX: The Psychological Corporation.
28. Wilson, B. A., Alderman, N., Burgess, P. W., Emslie, H., & Evans, J. J. (1996). *Behavioural Assessment of the Dysexecutive Syndrome.* Bury St Edmunds, UK: Harcourt Assessment.
29. Robertson, J. H., Ward, A., Ridgeway, V., & Nimmo-Smith, I. (1996). Test of everyday attention. *Journal of the International Neurological Society* 2: 525–534. doi:10.1017/s1355617700001697.
30. Warrington, E. K. & James, M. (1991) *The Visual Object and Space Perception Battery.* Bury St. Edmunds, UK: Thames Valley Test Company.
31. Whiting, S., Lincoln, N. B., Bhavnani, G., & Cockburn, J. (1985). *The Rivermead Perceptual Assessment Battery.* Windsor: NFER.
32. Bishop, D. (2003). *Test for Reception of Grammar, Version 2* (TROG-2). Pearson UK.

33. Dunn, L. M., Dunn, L. M., Whetton, C., & Pintilie, D. (1982). *British Picture Vocabulary Scale.* Windsor: NFER.
34. Sherer, M. (2004). *The Awareness Questionnaire.* Santa Clara Valley CA: Center for Outcome Measurement in Brain Injury.
35. Marin, R. S., Biedrzycki, R. C., & Firinciogullari, S. (1991). *Apathy Evaluation Scale (AES, AES-C, AES-I, AES-S).* Pittsburgh PA: University of Pittsburgh.
36. von Steinbüchel, N., Wilson, L., Gibbons, H., Hawthorne, G., Höfer, S., Schmidt, S., ... & Truelle, J. L. (2010). Quality of Life after Brain Injury (QOLIBRI): Scale validity and correlates of quality of life. *Journal of neurotrauma* 27(7): 1157–1165. doi:10.1089/neu.2009.1077.
37. Cuthill, F. M., Espie, C. A., & Cooper, S. A. (2003). Development and psychometric properties of the Glasgow Depression Scale for people with a learning disability: Individual and carer supplement versions. *The British Journal of Psychiatry* 182(4): 347–353. doi:10.1192/bjp.182.4.347.
38. Mindham, J. & Espie, C. A. (2003). Glasgow Anxiety Scale for people with an Intellectual Disability (GAS-ID): Development and psychometric properties of a new measure for use with people with mild intellectual disability. *Journal of Intellectual Disability Research* 47(1): 22–30. doi:10.1046/j.1365-2788.2003.00457.x.

5 Developmental Language Disorder

Kayleigh Wain

SPEECH AND LANGUAGE THERAPIST

Introduction

Developmental Language Disorder is a lifelong condition which falls under the umbrella of **neurodivergence**. It is a condition which is characterised by difficulty with language; both **comprehension** and **expression**, in the absence of other diagnosed conditions such as autism or Learning Disability (LD). Please see the relevant chapters for further information. Developmental Language Disorder is primarily diagnosed in childhood and is treated by Speech and Language Therapists. However, due to the complex nature of the disorder it may remain undiagnosed during a child's transition into adulthood.

The condition now known as Developmental Language Disorder has undergone several changes in terminology over the years: 'Specific Language Disorder', 'Specific Language Impairment', 'Developmental Language Impairment' and 'Language Disorder' all being terms to which this condition has been assigned in the past. Bishop et al. [1] conducted a review of the terminology in 2016 and ruled out alternative terminology for **Developmental Language Disorder** for a variety of reasons such as (1) there is little research to definitively state that the condition is caused by a delay versus disorder, (2) the term 'specific' implied that there were no other comorbidities, which often was not the case. Clinicians and researchers have also suggested that there is '*no perfect term*' to describe this collection of characteristics, given the wide variety of presentations. Therefore, Developmental Language Disorder was agreed upon by experts within the field. This chapter is primarily designed to introduce the condition and signpost the reader to different resources and information, rather than being a comprehensive clinical overview. It is always important to consider individual needs, aetiology, cooccurring conditions and gain a full clinical overview of the person.

DOI: 10.4324/9781003510659-5

This chapter is divided into the following sections:

Background

Function, cognition and progress in typically developing children is measured by **Developmental Milestones**. Developmental Milestones are measures of the 'typical' ages by which children achieve certain skills. Speech and language are important components of these milestones, alongside other skills such as fine and gross motor skills. Below details an outline of a typically developing child's speech, language and communication skills at the various milestones. You can find more information about developmental milestones on the Department for Education pages on the United Kingdom's government website [2].

Birth to 2–3 months

- Smiling
- Vocalising (e.g. 'ooo' 'ahh')
- Providing vocalisations when spoken to (e.g. 'oo')
- Crying to communicate basic needs
- Providing eye to eye contact
- Responding to voice by moving their heads

4 months

- Laughing and chuckling
- Anticipation of contact (e.g. increased response to human contact) (turning head, smiling)
- High pitched squeals and sounds

6 months

- Beginning to make simple consonant/vowel sounds (e.g. 'da' 'ga')

9 months

- Copying single sounds
- Babbling (e.g. 'dada')
- Beginning to comprehend simple commands (e.g. 'give that to me')
- Beginning to comprehend familiar single words (e.g. biscuit, book)

12 months +

- A small vocabulary (e.g. mama, dada)
- Babbling to form close approximations of single words (e.g. 'din' for target 'drink')
- Beginning to look at picture books for two to three minutes with support
- Understanding of some single words and commands within the context of routines (e.g. 'bath-time' 'bed')

18 months–24 months

- Comprehension of two stage commands (e.g. 'give me the drink and the book')
- Vocabulary develops to approximately 50 words
- Comprehension of most familiar single words (around 200 to 500 words)
- Beginning to make two-word utterances for a variety of communicative purposes (e.g. 'drink please' 'hi doggy')
- The child has mostly developed their 'frontal' speech sounds (e.g. 't, d, w, m' (sounds that are made at the front of the mouth))

2–3 years

- Listening to and remembering simple stories with pictures.
- Understanding longer instructions, such as 'make teddy jump' or 'where's mummy's coat?'
- Understanding simple 'who', 'what' and 'where' questions.
- Vocabulary has increased to 300 words
- Putting four or five words together to make short sentences, such as 'want more juice' or 'he took my ball'.

- Using action words as well as nouns, such as 'run' and 'fall'.
- Starting to use simple plurals by adding 's', for example 'shoes' or 'cars'.

The milestones outlined above are fairly typical in terms of development; however, there can be conditions other than Developmental Language Disorder that can impact on progress, for example Attention Deficit Hyperactivity Disorder (ADHD), autism and LD.

The definition of Developmental Language Disorder is that there is a **significant delay/disorder** in the child's language ability **across modalities** without a pre-existing neurological condition which can determine the aetiology of the condition. This means the child has significant difficulty with their language skills but is not diagnosed with another neurodevelopmental condition. Current research suggests that Developmental Language Disorder affects up to 7% of the population [3]. Developmental Language Disorder is a lesser-known form of neurodivergence. The Royal College of Speech and Language Therapists alongside other providers are beginning to raise more awareness of the disorder [4].

Developmental Language Disorder is defined within the Diagnostic and Statistical Manual (fifth edition-TR) [5] as the following. There is still ongoing research and discussions to determine the exact definition of Developmental Language Disorder. However, these are the current diagnostic criteria:

A. **Persistent difficulties in the acquisition and use of language across modalities** (i.e. spoken, written, sign language, or other), due to deficits in comprehension or production that include the following:

- Reduced vocabulary (word knowledge and use).
- Limited sentence structure (ability to put words and word endings together to form sentences based on the rules of grammar and morphology).
- Impairments in discourse (ability to use vocabulary and connect sentences to explain or describe a topic or series of events or have a conversation).

B. **Language abilities are substantially and quantifiably below those expected for age**, resulting in functional limitations in effective communication, social participation, academic achievement, or occupational performance, individually or in any combination.

C. Onset of symptoms is in the **early developmental period.**
D. The difficulties are **not attributable to hearing or other sensory impairment, motor dysfunction, or another medical or neurological condition and are not better explained by intellectual disability (intellectual developmental disorder) or global developmental delay.**

Note: The conceptualisation in ICD-11 demonstrates slight differences to that in the DSM. 'Developmental Language Disorders' within this framework falls under 'developmental speech or language disorders', which is part of the neurodevelopmental disorders' domain. Whilst similarities exist across the two diagnostic tools, (e.g. severity of impairment), the ICD-11 provides a less broad but more detailed framework offering the opportunity to specify explicit subtypes of expressive, receptive and mixed language difficulties.

When Developmental Language Disorder is thought to be potentially relevant to an individual, it is crucial to consider communication developmental milestones to determine *when* the onset of their difficulty with language occurred. As defined above, it can only be categorised as Developmental Language Disorder if the difficulty began to occur in the early developmental period.

Another essential step in the process of considering whether a child has Developmental Language Disorder is to fully explore other **risk factors** for delayed language development. For example, a child should have their hearing assessed by an audiologist to determine if there is any hearing loss, as hearing loss can have a significant impact upon a child's ability to learn new language and speech sounds. In the United Kingdom, screening typically takes place when the child is a newborn and then is revisited by a Health Visitor early in the child's development. Despite these previous assessments, it is important that clinicians review this in order to rule this out where developmental language disorder is suspected.

This condition is also classed as being '… across modalities …' meaning that there is no specific area of language that is affected; rather, it will impact many domains of language for the child, such as their reading, writing, spoken language and their comprehension of language.

As previously set out, the typically developing child has around 300 words in their everyday vocabulary by the age of two to three years. For children with Developmental Language Disorder, it is likely that this number is substantially reduced at this age. They may experience difficulties with engagement, and their ability to follow commands will often fall substantially short of what is expected. In addition, where a child is unable to express themselves reliably or comprehend commands from their caregivers, this can impact on their quality of life and can lead to delays in them achieving additional developmental milestones. In turn, the child may become increasingly frustrated with these limitations and, as a consequence, may begin to display behaviours that challenge.

In addition to this, due to the difficulty experienced with language, the child may find themselves at a disadvantage in regard to both educational and social opportunities. Part of the typically developing child's trajectory involves them beginning to play with other children in settings such as nurseries and playgroups, where imaginative play is crucial to the development of additional skills such as negotiation, role play and contributing to the development of **theory of mind** (please see Chapter 3 on autism for further information). The child with Developmental Language Disorder often experiences difficulties in fully participating in activities such as these, as the play is often accompanied by a narrative of the type of play that is occurring, which is compromised in these children.

Within educational settings, the child will often begin to fall behind their typically developing peers associated with their Developmental Language Disorder. Language is crucial to accessing all aspects of the education syllabus, therefore in the absence of typically acquired core language skills at appropriate milestones, the child will have difficulty learning new skills and information. As previously mentioned, whilst Developmental Language Disorder is excluded should the child meet criteria for intellectual development disorder, the nature of the disorder means it is considered a risk factor for other conditions such as dyslexia or LD [6]. If a child has undiagnosed Developmental Language Disorder they could potentially fall behind their peers in terms of reading, writing and learning ability. This means it is crucial to source extra support in educational settings.

Whilst Bishop et al. [7] have carried out a plethora of research into Developmental Language Disorder, it still remains an under-researched condition and a priority for future projects. It is noted within their research that the aetiology of the disorder remains disputed as a large proportion of the children diagnosed with this condition are hypothesised to have multifactorial causes. For example, genetic predisposition may make it more likely to have Developmental Language Disorder.

Heterogeneity within language disorders?

As previously discussed, children are believed to be at a greater risk for Developmental Language Disorder if there is a family history of neurodivergence. The aetiology of the disorder is multifactorial, meaning that there are various difficulties that can co-occur and that can lead to a child experiencing difficulties with language.

It is widely recognised that within Developmental Language Disorder there is a diverse range of clinical presentations. Whilst some children may experience a mild language delay i.e. a year after the typical milestones, others may experience a severe difficulty with language that impedes on all communication associated with activities of daily living. The diversity of the disorder is one of the reasons underpinning the ongoing debate regarding the definition of Developmental Language Disorder [8].

Despite the varying degrees of Developmental Language Disorder, there are various considerations in regard to diversity within the disorder.

Sex

It has been found that males are more likely than females to be diagnosed with Developmental Language Disorder. There is evidence to suggest that females are able to compensate better than males due to differences in working memory and cognitive processes [9].

Bilingualism

Whilst bilingualism in itself is not a risk factor for Developmental Language Disorder, bilingual children's milestones typically occur later than a monolingual child, such that there can be difficulties acquiring a diagnosis. There may also be cultural factors that lead to parents in some cultures to seek support later than others. It has been suggested that bilingual children with Developmental Language Disorder may present with more severe language disorder [10]. Bilingualism may contribute to **diagnostic overshadowing** due to the often-delayed developmental milestones of bilingual children.

Genetics

Studies suggest that there is a higher incidence of Developmental Language Disorder if a child has a neurodivergent parent or a sibling with a condition such as Developmental Language Disorder, autism or Attention Hyperactivity Disorder [11].

Mental health

Due to the challenges that language difficulties can present to a child in developing social relationships, providing narratives (storytelling) and using language to connect with people, it has been recognised that children and adults with Developmental Language Disorder may subsequently experience difficulties with their mental health [12]. In order to access the basic human need of connecting with others, storytelling is essential. If an individual experiences challenges with accessing language in order to form a narrative, this can lead to exclusion from everyday activities that strengthen an individual's ability to participate in society. Challenges may occur in developing friendships, accessing talking therapies and other public services to support mental health.

Education

Children and adults with a diagnosis of Developmental Language Disorder experience difficulties participating in formal education [3]. An assessment of a person's needs by educators, psychologists and Speech and Language Therapists is recommended in order that additional support, such as information being presented visually or increased time made available when completing examinations, can be set out in a person-centred plan.

Socio-economic status

As a child develops into adulthood, activities such as going to work, handling money and liaison with services, all continue to present challenges to individuals with Developmental Language Disorder. A person's work opportunities may be limited to physical work, which may have a direct impact on the individual's socio-economic status. In some cases, an individual may have limitations that negate engagement in employment all together due to the many barriers that they may face in participating in work associated with the demands on language (e.g. training, using computer systems).

Quality of life

As stated, individuals with Developmental Language Disorder may find it difficult to connect with others and in turn may be at an increased risk of victimisation [13]. This can further compromise an individual's quality of life.

Developmental Language Disorder is a lifelong condition which can have functional, emotional and social implications throughout an individual's life trajectory. For example, as an adult, difficulties with language may be linked to problems with financial literacy, which may in turn impede an individual's ability to reach their potential in society [14].

Justice system

Many individuals within the justice system experience speech, language and communication disorders. The nature of Developmental Language Disorder means that some young people/adults may find it difficult to navigate social situations and may be vulnerable to peer pressure associated with poorly developed language skills; this may be a contributing factor to their pathway into criminal activity [15].

(|▶) Things to look out for

Developmental Language Disorder may present similarly to other neurodivergent conditions such as autism, ADHD or LD. The condition can also co-occur alongside dyslexia, making it difficult to differentially diagnose.

There are several observable signs of Developmental Language Disorder that may give rise to diagnosis and support a clinician to form a picture of an individual's communication needs.

Language difficulties

- An individual's ability to form sentences, find words and to comprehend instructions.
- An individual may find it difficult to tell a story (narrative production).
- Sentences may sound unfinished, or the individual may use different grammar to that which the listener is expecting.
- The individual may appear to be defiant or unwilling to complete instructions if they are overwhelmed by information.

- The person might not use words consistent with their age/experience level. They may require support with reading and writing.

Behaviour changes

- May occur in younger children and/or young adults (especially if they have remained undiagnosed and have not received support).
- The individual may be observed not to follow commands or instructions.
- The person may have difficulty sticking to routines or attending school due to them finding these tasks/contexts challenging.
- Some individuals may have contact with the criminal justice system.
- The individual may be isolated, may lack social circles, and/or may be the victim of abuse.
- Children and adults may find it hard to pay attention to information.

Screening assessments

When determining whether Developmental Language Disorder is present, it is important to take a full and comprehensive developmental history of the individual. This should be completed where possible with their full-time caregivers/guardians and other stakeholders such as social workers, Educational Psychologists, teachers and/or nursery nurses. Comprehensive information should be gathered regardless of the individual's age when determining the presence of neurodivergence. The relevant information to gather should include:

- Prenatal and postnatal presentation of the mother and child
- Presence of other diagnoses
- Presence of trauma
- Whether developmental milestones were achieved
- How they behave within different settings
- Current medication
- Functions of communication (e.g. how they are currently communicating)
- Means, reasons and opportunities for communication [16]
- Monolingualism vs bilingualism
- Presence of neurodivergence within the family
- Assessments completed by paediatricians/psychologists
- How difficulties impact the individual

As of yet there are no commonly used, or widely known, formal screening assessments for Developmental Language Disorder. Assessment and diagnosis are usually completed by a Speech and Language Therapist and/or Educational Psychologist.

Specialist assessment

A Speech and Language Therapist may diagnose Developmental Language Disorder following assessment, observation and consultation with the individual and their family. The Speech and Language Therapist will also work closely with Educational Psychologists to form a clinical picture of the child/individual's history and cognitive functioning. Consultation with paediatricians, health visitors and nurses will assist in determining the nature of any comorbidities and whether this needs to be factored into the diagnostic/formulation process.

The Speech and Language Therapist may benefit from completing the following after conducting a full case history.

- An observation of the child/individual in their regular settings (e.g. an educational establishment)
- An interview or session with the child/individual to observe their language informally (comprehension, expression, reading, writing)
- Formal assessment to determine the nature of difficulty with language

Speech and Language Therapists have a variety of formal assessments that can support a diagnosis of Developmental Language Delay; however, there is not a single diagnostic tool that provides this; rather, this information is usually used in conjunction with informal assessment, observations and a full case history.

Clinical assessments

There are a variety of clinical assessments for language available, which are set out below, albeit this list is not exhaustive.

- **Auditory Skills Assessment [17] – Donna Geffner, Ph.D. and Ronald Goldman, Ph.D.** ASA^{TM} is a tool for early identification of young children who might be at risk for auditory skill deficits and/or early literacy skill difficulties. This screen provides accurate, developmentally based results to help determine which children may need follow-up, intervention, or further evaluation.
- **Children's Communication Checklist CC-2 [18]** – screens for communication problems in children aged 4 to 16 years.
- Clinical Evaluation of Language Fundamentals Preschool-3 UK [19]. CELF Preschool-3 UK – Elisabeth H. Wiig, Ph.D., Wayne A.

Secord, Ph.D., Eleanor Semel, Ed.D. – assesses aspects of language necessary for preschool children to meet the language demands of the classroom.

- **Clinical Evaluation of Language Fundamentals - Fourth Edition UK** [20]. CELF-4 UK. Eleanor Semel, Ed.D., Elisabeth H. Wiig, Ph.D., Wayne A. Secord, Ph.D. – Evaluates the nature and extent of language difficulties in school children and adolescents with CELF-4 UK.
- **Expression, Reception and Recall of Narrative Instrument – ERRNI** [21]. Dorothy Bishop, Ph.D. – assesses the ability to relate, comprehend and remember a story after a delay.
- **Test for Reception of Grammar. TROG-2** [22]. **Dorothy Bishop, Ph.D.** – measures an individual's understanding of grammatical contrasts. Tests understanding of 20 constructs four times each using different test stimuli.

Adaptations and considerations

✓ Use short, clear and simple language.

✓ Provide information in an **easy read** format with images and symbols to support an individual's comprehension and understanding.

✓ Observe the individual across settings (e.g. school and the home environment), particularly their reading, writing, narrative skills and their ability to respond to commands.

✓ Gather the views of parents and professionals about the individual's strengths and needs.

✓ Consider the individual's language skills in the context of their individual needs (e.g. their personality, other diagnoses, their social skills, play and participation in activities of daily living whilst considering their typical cultural and socio-economic norms).

✓ A Speech and Language Therapist and Educational Psychologist and/ or Clinical Psychologist referral should be made if Developmental Language Disorder is suspected.

Signposting

It seems that often little is known about Developmental Language Disorder in the wider public domain. It may be that it remains unrecognised by the general public due to it being a '**hidden disability**' and due to its similarities to other neurodivergent conditions such as ADHD or autism, which themselves have only begun to be better recognised in the last few decades. Individual researchers such as Dorothy Bishop have conducted studies, campaigning and research to bring about more awareness of the disorder.

There are a large number of support services to help individuals and their families with Developmental Language Disorder both in the UK and further afield. It is recommended you seek support if you or your child have been newly diagnosed or suspect the disorder is present. In the first instance you should contact your GP and ask for a referral to Speech and Language Therapy. Due to the disparity in provision of services within the UK and a national shortage of Speech and Language Therapists, some individuals may seek support privately dependent on their circumstances.

- **RADLD – Raising Awareness of Developmental Language Disorder.**[1] Previously called the RALLI campaign, their mission is to increase awareness of Developmental Language Disorder.
- **RCSLT – Royal College of Speech and Language Therapists.**[2] The main body for Speech and Language Therapists in the United Kingdom has clinical information and advice regarding Developmental Language Disorder.
- **The DLD Project**[3] is an Australian project to provide evidence-based information on Developmental Language Disorder.
- **DLD and Me**[4] is a project based in the USA which aims to raise awareness of the disorder and offer relevant resources.
- **ASLTIP – Association of Speech and Language Therapists in Independent Practice**[5] is an independent body for Speech and Language Therapists in private practice in the United Kingdom, whose technical skills and specialisms are signposted on the website.
- **ASHA – American Speech-Language-Hearing Association**[6] is a Body for Speech and Language Pathologists in the United States of America. The website has resources and information on Developmental Language Disorder.
- **Communicourt**[7] are communication specialists who work on behalf of His Majesty's Courts and Tribunal Service (HMCTS) to support people during their court proceedings.

Michael case examples

Michael is a 16-year-old boy who has just finished school. He has a good sense of humour but is also shy. He found school challenging and often missed classes; he reported how he 'couldn't wait to leave school'. Despite not having enjoyed school, Michael was very good in practical classes where he did not have to rely on verbal instructions, such as woodwork, and design work such as soldering, although he would often get into trouble for leaving his equipment in dangerous positions. Michael did not attend his GCSE examinations despite encouragement from his teachers, therefore he received an ungraded mark for the five GCSEs that he was entered for. Michael received pupil support regularly throughout his schooling and he was often 'on report' where he had to check in with senior teachers at the school. As Michael often did not attend his lessons and he displayed verbal and physical aggression when he did attend, the school labelled him as a 'challenging pupil' and he was warned that he would be expelled unless he could improve his behaviour within school. Despite the challenging behaviour, Michael's design teachers thought that he would benefit from attending college to undertake an apprenticeship in joinery and they encouraged him to do so; they believed it would help him with behaviour management. Michael's favourite teacher, Mr Ross, discussed this with Michael throughout his final year of school. Mr Ross noted that when Michael was discussing his future plans, he would use immature language, and he did not appear able to express himself fully. Mr Ross believed this was due to Michael being shy.

Over the summer prior to starting college, Michael made some new friends in the local youth centre. They encouraged him to start hanging around in the city centre with them, listening to music, going into the shops and fast-food restaurants. At first, Michael was very shy and quiet, however he gained more confidence and began interacting with larger groups of people than he had ever done previously. Unfortunately, his new friends had ulterior motives, soon realised that Michael was somewhat vulnerable and was open to manipulation, and got Michael to do whatever they wanted him to. Michael did not appear to understand situations the way that his peers did. One day, they bumped into a rival gang in a fast-food restaurant on the high street. The other boys gave Michael a knife and asked him to 'off' the boy they were pointing at. Michael had never really developed the social awareness skills that would equip him to deal with complex situations such as this, and he lacked the confidence to say no. This was also the first time Michael had felt that he belonged to a social group, so he felt the need to impress his friends. Michael used the weapon against the rival gang member, causing life-long damage and injury to the victim.

When Michael was questioned at the police station, the officers were confused. Michael used odd language and did not really appear to understand their questions. Michael appeared different from other boys of his age. The officers were unsure of Michael's capacity and therefore asked the Mental Health Services to conduct a review of his abilities. A Registered Mental Health Nurse, Joan, visited Michael and was also concerned about his language abilities and referred Michael to a Speech and Language Therapist. The assessment took a while to take place due to a lack of Speech and Language Therapists in Michael's area; however, he was seen for assessment prior to his trial. The Speech and Language Therapist discovered that Michael did indeed have Developmental Language Disorder, however this had not been identified during his schooling for a variety of reasons: Michael's shyness, behaviour, attendance, lack of family input and his ability to mask his limitations in classes that he enjoyed. The assessment found that Michael was able to comprehend single sentences with **up to three information carrying words** (key words such as nouns and verbs). If long streams of information were provided in a paragraph, Michael comprehended the last piece of information he heard and 'filled in the gaps' for the rest of the information, leading to misunderstandings. **Michael's expressive language, reading and writing ability was the equivalent to that of an 8-year-old.**

If Developmental Language Disorder had been identified earlier in Michael's life and he had received support for his needs, he may not have made the same choices as he did on that day.

Michael was sentenced to five years in prison for Grievous Bodily Harm (GBH). His Developmental Language Disorder was taken into account during the trial; Michael was provided with support from a Communicourt Speech and Language Therapist. In prison he received access to the Speech and Language Therapy he required and began to make good progress. He also began to train in joinery and build a career pathway for himself to pursue once he was released from prison.

Ava case examples

Ava is a 4-year-old child. Her parents were very concerned that she was still not meeting her speech and language milestones and referred her for an autism assessment. At 4 years old she was only saying single words and had still not developed speech sounds such as 'k' and 'g'. Ava's nursery was also concerned as they noted that Ava was very quiet during playtime and would often play on her own. Ava was assessed by an Educational Psychologist and Speech and Language Therapist in her home and at nursery. The assessors were looking for evidence of the 'triad of impairment' to see if Ava had an autism diagnosis. However, the only signs of neurodivergence they could find were the speech and language delay. Ava had some challenging behaviour associated with her delay, likely related to frustration at being unable to communicate her basic needs. However, there were no signs of autism such as rigid and repetitive behaviours, fixed interests or difficulty with social interaction. It appeared that Ava wanted to play with the other children but that she did not have the language skills to do so.

The Speech and Language Therapist carried out further specific speech and language assessments to establish the nature of the speech and language delay fully. The SLT also asked the parents to arrange other assessments, such as a hearing test for Ava. The assessment found that Ava had Developmental Language Disorder and was almost three years behind her milestone trajectory. Ava had difficulty with forming two-word phrases and difficulty with specific speech sounds such as 'k'. Ava was able to name some familiar objects but sometimes made mistakes with the sounds required for the words.

As Ava's Developmental Language Disorder was identified early, she was able to access regular Speech and Language Therapy sessions through the NHS, where support for her family and 1:1 treatment to target nouns and verbs were provided. Ava also practised her speech sounds with the SLT. The SLT provided homework to Ava's parents so that she could practise her speech and language at home with them too.

When Ava turned 5 years old she started primary school. At this point she had received 9 months of Speech and Language Therapy. She was provided with an Education and Health Care Plan (EHCP), which outlined her needs and how teachers could support her with her development. Ava was assigned a Teaching Assistant to sit with her in class and go over the syllabus on a 1:1 basis. Ava had finished her course of NHS provided Speech and Language Therapy with ongoing recommendations provided, therefore Ava's parents used the ASLTIP website for independent SLTs for extra support.

When Ava turned 10 years old she began her final year of primary school. With the additional support of SLT and her parents fully engaging in the recommendations, Ava had developed her speech and language to the equivalent of a 7-year-old. Ava continued to have 1:1 support in the school setting, and progressed to mainstream secondary education, where her EHCP remained in place to outline the support she required.

Notes

1 RADLD (n.d.). RADLD – Raising Awareness of Developmental Language Disorder. [online] RADLD. Available at: https://radld.org/.
2 Royal College of Speech and Language Therapists (2019). RCSLT Home. [online] Royal College of Speech and Language Therapists. Available at: https://www.rcslt.org/.
3 The DLD Project. (n.d.). The DLD Project. Information, resources & training. [online] Available at: https://thedldproject.com/.
4 Kevin (2008). DLD | Developmental Language Disorder | Language Disorder. [online] DLD and Me. Available at: https://dldandme.org/.
5 ASLTIP. (n.d.). Speech and Language Therapy. Public Support & Information. [online] Available at: https://asltip.com/.
6 ASHA (2019). American Speech-Language-Hearing Association | ASHA. [online] Asha.org. Available at: https://www.asha.org/.
7 Communicourt. https://www.communicourt.co.uk/

References

1. Bishop, D.V., Snowling, M.J., Thompson, P.A. & Greenhalgh, T. (2017). Phase 2 of CATALISE: A multinational and multidisciplinary Delphi consensus study of problems with language development: Terminology. *Journal of Child Psychology and Psychiatry and Allied Disciplines*, 58(10). doi:10.1111/jcpp.12721.
2. Department for Education (2023). Development matters. [online]. Retrieved from: https://www.gov.uk/government/publications/development-matters–2/development-matters.
3. Erisman, M. C. & Blom, E. (2020). Reading outcomes in children with developmental language disorder: A person-centered approach. *Autism & Developmental Language Impairments*, 5. doi:10.1177/2396941520979857.
4. RCSLT (2023). A vision for Developmental Language Disorder (DLD) for the UK. [online] Retrieved from: https://www.rcslt.org/wp-content/uploads/2023/10/A-Vision-for-Developmental-Language-Disorder.pdf.
5. American Psychiatric Association. (2022). *Diagnostic and Statistical Manual of Mental Disorders* (5th ed., text rev.) American Psychiatric Association.
6. Kevin (2008). DLD | Developmental Language Disorder | Language Disorder. [online] DLD and me. Retrieved from: https://dldandme.org/.
7. Bishop, D. V. M. (1992). The underlying nature of specific language impairment. *Journal of Child Psychology and Psychiatry*, 33(1), 3–66. doi:10.1111/j.1469-7610.1992.tb00858.x.
8. Botting, N., Bean-Ellawadi, A. & Williams, D. (2016). Language impairments in childhood: A range of profiles, a variety of reasons. *Autism & Developmental Language Impairments*, 1, doi:10.1177/2396941516654609.
9. McGregor, K. K., Arbisi-Kelm, T., Eden, N., & Oleson, J. (2020). The word learning profile of adults with developmental language disorder. *Autism & Developmental Language Impairments*, 5, doi:10.1177/2396941519899311.

10. Crutchley, A., Botting, N., & Conti-Ramsden, G. (1997). Bilingualism and specific language impairment in children attending language units. *International Journal of Language and Communication Disorders*, 32(2), 267–276. doi:10.3109/13682829709020409.

11. Botting, N., Bean-Ellawadi, A., & Williams, D. M. (2016). Language impairments in childhood: A range of profiles, a variety of reasons. *Autism & Developmental Language Impairments*, 1. doi:10.1177/2396941516654609.

12. Hobson, H., Kalsi, M., Cotton, L., Forster, M., & Toseeb, U. (2022). Supporting the mental health of children with speech, language and communication needs: The views and experiences of parents. *Autism & Developmental Language Impairments*, 7. doi:10.1177/23969415221101137.

13. Wadman, R., Botting, N., Durkin, K., & Conti-Ramsden, G. (2011). Changes in emotional health symptoms in adolescents with specific language impairment. *International Journal of Language and Communication Disorders*, 46(6), 641–656. doi:10.1111/j.1460–6984.2011.00033.x.

14. Winstanley, M., Durkin, K., Webb, R. T., & Conti-Ramsden, G. (2018). Financial capability and functional financial literacy in young adults with developmental language disorder. *Autism & Developmental Language Impairments*, 3. doi:10.1177/2396941518794500.

15. Bryan, K. (2004). Preliminary study of the prevalence of speech and language difficulties in young offenders. *International Journal of Language and Communication Disorders*, 39(3), 391–400. doi:10.1080/13682820410001666376.

16. Money, D. (1997). A comparison of three approaches to delivering a speech and language therapy service to people with learning disabilities. *International Journal of Language & Communication Disorders*, 32(4), 449–466. doi:10.3109/13682829709082259.

17. www.pearsonclinical.co.uk. (n.d.). Auditory skills assessment. Retrieved from: https://www.pearsonclinical.co.uk/store/ukassessments/en/Store/Professional-Assessments/Developmental-Early-Childhood/School-Readiness/Auditory-Skills-Assessment/p/P100009067.html?tab=product-details.

18. www.pearsonclinical.co.uk. (n.d.). Children's communication checklist. Retrieved from: https://www.pearsonclinical.co.uk/store/ukassessments/en/c/Children%27s-Communication-Checklist/p/P100009204.html?tab=product-details.

19. www.pearsonclinical.co.uk. (n.d.). Clinical evaluation of language fundamentals preschool-3 uk. Retrieved from: https://www.pearsonclinical.co.uk/store/ukassessments/en/Store/Professional-Assessments/Developmental-Early-Childhood/Clinical-Evaluation-of-Language-Fundamentals-Preschool-3-UK/p/P100072000.html.

20. www.pearsonclinical.co.uk. (n.d.). *Clinical Evaluation of Language Fundamentals – Fourth Edition UK.* [online] Retrieved from: https://www.pearsonclinical.co.uk/store/ukassessments/en/Store/Professional-Assessments/Speech-%26-Language/Clinical-Evaluation-of-Language-Fundamentals—Fourth-Edition-UK/p/P100009283.html.

21. www.pearsonclinical.co.uk. (n.d.). Expression, reception and recall of narrative instrument. Retrieved from: https://www.pearsonclinical.co.uk/store/uka

ssessments/en/Store/Professional-Assessments/Speech-%26-Language/Literacy/
Expression%2C-Reception-and-Recall-of-Narrative-Instrument/p/P100009217.
html.

22. www.pearsonclinical.co.uk. (n.d.). Test for reception of grammar.
Retrieved from: https://www.pearsonclinical.co.uk/store/ukassessments/en/
Store/Professional-Assessments/Speech-%26-Language/Vocabulary/Test-for-Re
ception-of-Grammar/p/P100009232.html.

6 Executive functioning

Sarah Ashworth-Watts

CONSULTANT FORENSIC PSYCHOLOGIST

Introduction

Executive function is the name for a collection of thinking skills that we use when solving problems, making decisions, planning, completing tasks, and reflecting on what we have done. We rely on many of these executive function skills on a daily basis, such as when we are cooking a meal, following a conversation between our friends, interacting with family members, completing tasks required of us at work, studying for an exam and even planning our day. As such, impairment of the executive functions can have a significant effect on many aspects of everyday living and can impact upon the quality of someone's life. It can be helpful to think of your executive functioning system as your control centre, or navigational system. A good metaphor would be to imagine this system as the air traffic control tower of the brain, monitoring and directing the travel of planes.

We should remember that executive function disorder is *not* a specific stand-alone diagnosis or condition. Instead, many neurological, psychiatric, psychological, and behavioural disorders can affect a person's executive functioning.

This chapter aims to provide an overview of what executive functions are, what may affect someone's ability to perform tasks requiring these skills, and how a clinician may go about screening for and assessing these skills in order to make appropriate adaptations and adjustments to their practice.

This chapter is divided into the following sections:

1 Background
2 Heterogeneity associated with executive function
3 Things to look out for
4 Screening assessments
5 Specialist assessment

DOI: 10.4324/9781003510659-6

Background

The executive functions are a set of processes essential for the cognitive control of behaviour. This includes selecting and successfully monitoring behaviours that facilitate the attainment of identified goals.

These functions include three important cognitive processes:

- **Cognitive and behavioural inhibition** relates to being able to ignore distractions (internal and external) and to resist an urge to do something.
- **Working memory** involves the ability to hold and manipulate information in your mind, in order to use it in some way.
- **Mental flexibility** relates to being able to consciously change your thinking or think about more than one thing at the same time.

Higher-order executive functions require the simultaneous use of multiple basic functions and include planning, and **fluid intelligence** (e.g. reasoning and problem-solving). People start to acquire these skills during childhood, but these continue to develop well into the twenties.

There are eight general skills which rely upon effective executive functioning.

- **Emotional control** is the ability to modulate or manage emotions and feelings. If someone struggles with this, their emotions can be repressed or not experienced, limiting the awareness or access the person has to them. Problems with this can also reduce the effectiveness of talking therapies until some degree of emotional understanding is developed. This can be enhanced by developing the individual's understanding of the physiological manifestations of emotional experience (**mind–body connection**). Someone may use this skill when trying not to get too angry during an argument with a family member.
- **Inhibition** relates to the ability to control one's own thoughts and behaviours. For people who experience problems within this area, their actions occur before, or without conscious access to the thought that produced the action (e.g. doing without thinking). The impulsive action is experienced as if it has come out of nowhere for

the individual, because it is not consciously processed. Again, interventions which strengthen the mind–body connection can slow this process down and allow for skill application to better manage automatic responses. Someone may use this skill when trying not to make an inappropriate joke with their colleague whilst at work!

- **Working memory** is comprised of several types of memory that all work together. This includes visual memory (memory for things we have seen), visual memory manipulation (being able to adapt or change things 'in our mind'), auditory memory (memory for things we have heard), and spatial memory (memory for things in relation to space and location). This also involves the ability to hold information in conscious thought, manipulate and have access to it for immediate use. Someone may use this skill when adding up the cost of a shopping list.

- **Initiation** relates to the ability to initiate, or start, a task. Individuals can experience difficulties with initiation for many reasons (e.g. apathy, motivation, anxiety, perfectionism). The process of initiation can be accomplished either by external cueing from others (e.g. when someone tells someone else to start a task) or internal cueing by the self (i.e. self-initiation). Someone may use this skill when trying to get their homework started!

- **Planning** is the process of thinking about the activities required to achieve an identified goal. This skill relies upon visual memory (e.g. picturing what we want to achieve) and visual memory manipulation (e.g. considering how each step can get us closer to the goal). This might often operate below the level of consciousness; however, for more complex or long-term tasks, it may be brought into conscious awareness. For individuals who experience planning deficits, consciously developing these skills may be needed before the process becomes more automatic. For example, someone may use this skill when starting a diet, thinking about which foods they wish to cut out (e.g. when they go shopping), how much exercise they need to do and what this may involve (e.g. gym membership), will they join a weight loss club and what financial implications this may have, what changes they need to make to their lifestyle (e.g. will they quit drinking when they go out at a weekend), and so on.

- **Organisation** is the process of applying a specific system to a developed plan. It involves keeping track of activities, categorising, and prioritising tasks. This skill requires working memory in order to hold this information in mind and then to use it effectively. Someone may use this skill when trying to cook a meal from a new recipe, getting all the items and equipment together.

- **Self-monitoring** is the ability to reflect upon and assess one's own performance. It involves an individual's ability to connect past knowledge with present experiences in a way that allows the person to plan, organise, strategie, attend, and manage time. Someone may use this skill when thinking back to a job interview where they were unsuccessful.
- **Shift** is the ability to be able to think and adjust one's behaviour as situations change (e.g. 'go with the flow'). This allows for responsive problem solving, being able to adapt in the face of unexpected difficulty and change plans in the light of challenges. Someone may use this skill when a train is cancelled and a replacement bus service is provided, and as such they need to amend their plans (e.g. let people know of any changes), manage their expectations (e.g. mode of transport, route, etc.) and adapt their behaviour (e.g. walk to the bus stop rather than the train station).

Heterogeneity associated with executive function

As we have learned, executive function disorder is not a diagnosis in or of itself, but rather it can be considered a symptom that occurs with conditions that disrupt the brain's ability to control thoughts, emotions, and behaviour. However, many conditions can impact a person's executive functions, and the profile may present differently depending on the condition that the person is experiencing.

Executive functioning deficits are common in **mental health conditions** such as depression, anxiety, bipolar disorder [1] and schizophrenia [2]. Specific domains of initiation, difficulties maintaining a goal, and cognitive inflexibility have been identified.

Many people with **neurodevelopmental differences**, such as autism, and Attention Deficit Hyperactivity Disorder (ADHD), also have differences in their thinking and learning, which may make some aspects of executive function easier and others harder. In autism, the domains of planning and flexibility have been found to be particularly difficult [3], whereas in ADHD the difficulties are often complex and combined with distractibility and working memory alterations [4].

Finally, people who have sustained an **acquired brain injury**, specifically those affecting the **prefrontal cortex** (PFC, the front part of the frontal lobe; see Chapter 4 on acquired brain injury for more detail) may find that their executive functions are impacted upon.

An individual's executive functioning skill may also vary dependent on context. For example, an individual might be able to get started (initiate) and focus for long periods on an activity that interests them (hyper-focus). However, if they find a task boring, or they are fatigued, they may find it more difficult to both get started and to pay or sustain attention. Executive functions can also change based on the environment that the individual is in. For example, if an individual is in a loud, busy environment it might be more difficult for them to manage their emotions, impulses, and/or attention (e.g. if a child's attention was captured by something that excited them, they may impulsively run away from their caregiver towards the item of interest without considering risk or other factors).

Further complicating the picture is a group of individuals with damage to their PFC, some of whom have been found to present as skilful within clinical interviews and to perform typically on traditional office-based assessments whilst simultaneously demonstrating limitations within the domain of adaptive functioning. Such impairments to skills of everyday life may include problems with decision-making, multitasking, and goal setting, and these may be masked by preserved language and communication skills and/or lack of insight. This is referred to as the **Frontal Lobe Paradox** [5] or the 'knowing–doing dissociation' [6]. For further information please see [7] and [8] for an overview and clinical considerations.

In summary, although executive dysfunction is not a formal diagnosis in and of itself, it is important that any deficits within this domain are assessed and included in an individual's executive functioning profile and formulation, as these functions are implicated in, and therefore can be impactful upon, a broad range of skills.

Things to look out for

As with the additional neurodivergent profiles described within this handbook, it is not always possible to ascertain that someone may be experiencing limitations in their executive functioning simply by looking at them. Indeed, as previously set out, these difficulties may not always be apparent across contexts, and individuals may be able to compensate for or mask their difficulties in some situations.

As with other clinical presentations, executive function skills can develop differently, and as a result, so too can the markers of executive dysfunction vary from person to person.

If an individual is experiencing executive function difficulties, you might expect to see some of the following markers:

- Frequently misplace or lose personal items, such as their phone, keys, paperwork, and work, or school materials.
- Often forget appointments, tasks, or things they must do.
- Find it difficult to make and stick to plans; they may often double book themselves or cancel last minute.
- Experience problems multitasking or trying to do several things at once, such as having conversations whilst driving, or taking notes during a meeting or class.
- Find it hard to stick to a schedule; they may become distracted or start completing things out of order.
- Have difficulty managing their time; they may turn up too late, or too early for appointments.
- Find it hard to come up with new ideas or ways to go about problems (**generation**); they may not be able to think of their own ideas and may copy others'.
- Find it challenging to get started on tasks (**initiation**); even for things they may want to do and are of value to them.
- Have difficulty keeping their personal spaces organised; they may have messy or disorganised offices, bedrooms, or homes in general.
- Find it challenging to navigate novel problems, frustrations, or setbacks; they may give up when faced with difficulties, or act in a way that is unlikely to be effective.
- Have difficulty remembering information or following instructions that involve multiple steps; for example, they may have trouble following directions that someone gives them to a place they have not previously visited, or following a new recipe.
- Find it hard to control their impulses; they may act on the spur of the moment without seeming to consider the consequences.
- Find it difficult to manage their emotions, which may impact upon their behaviour.
- Have trouble putting complex thoughts or abstract concepts into words (they may say things such as '*I don't know how to explain it*' or '*I can't find the right words to describe*").

Screening assessments

It is important to gather information about the person's history to see whether there is any evidence of difficulties with executive functioning. Further to this, as executive functioning difficulties are more likely to occur alongside certain conditions (e.g. ADHD), an understanding of the individual's diagnostic history will be helpful in considering whether it is likely that someone may struggle with their executive functioning or even present with executive dysfunction syndrome.

It will be important to explore whether someone has ever experienced difficulties with their mental health such as having experienced depression, schizophrenia, or having been diagnosed with a neurodevelopmental disorder such as autism, or ADHD, a degenerative disorder such as dementia or Huntington's Disease, or whether they have ever sustained an injury to their head, resulting in damage to their frontal lobe. Remember, just because someone does not have a diagnosis, it does not necessarily mean that they do not have the condition!

Whilst gathering information about a person's daily functioning helps us to better understand their overall functioning and any limitations that they experience, there are several screening tools that can be helpful to assist clinicians in structuring their thinking, and/or to provide information about an individual's ability to perform certain tasks.

It is important to remember that these screening instruments are NOT diagnostic and should always be interpreted by a clinician in conjunction with additional gathered data, including that from a thorough clinical history, risk factors, and medical investigations where appropriate. Additionally, there are some stipulations regarding the qualification level required to use some of the suggested instruments set out below; therefore, it is important to ensure that clinicians are familiar with any such requirements prior to utilising them.

- **The Dysexecutive Questionnaire (DEX)** [9] is part of the Behavioural Assessment of the Dysexecutive Syndrome (discussed further in the specialist assessment section of this chapter). It is a standardised self-report questionnaire that looks at possible behavioural changes an individual might present with as a result of a potential dysexecutive syndrome. There is also an informant version, which it is suggested is completed by someone who knows the individual well.
- **The FRONTIER Executive Screen (FES)** [10] is a brief screening test of executive functions. It looks specifically at the areas of fluency, inhibition, and working memory. It was designed to differentiate between fronto-temporal dementia and Alzheimer's disease (AD) which are conditions that tend to show different patterns of executive functioning difficulties. Higher scores are indicative of better executive functioning.

- **The Trail Making Test (TMT)** [11] is a short neuropsychological test that examines working memory, visual processing, visuospatial skills, selective and divided attention, processing speed, and psychomotor coordination. It involves completing two tasks under timed conditions, which can then be compared to normed cut-off data.

Specialist assessment

Executive dysfunction and executive function disorder are not official conditions listed in the Diagnostic and Statistical Manual of Mental Disorders (DSM-5), and as such a doctor or mental health professional will be unable to diagnose these conditions specifically. However, gathering an understanding of an individual's strengths and vulnerabilities, developing an executive functioning profile and generating a hypothesis as to the aetiology of such difficulties can be extremely beneficial for both the individual and the professionals working with them.

If the executive functioning difficulties are found to be the consequence of an injury or illness, as with a suspected brain injury, medical professionals may use **brain imaging technology** to evaluate the extent of the brain injury (see Chapter 4 on brain injury for more details about different types of scans). **Neuropsychological tests** are also used, which involve the individual being asked to perform specific tasks that utilise certain executive functions. Exploration of such deficits has demonstrated the need for **ecologically valid assessments**, that is, assessments which measure skills as applied in real life scenarios rather than sterile laboratory-based tasks. Some examples of commonly used tests are provided here:

- **The Multiple Errands Test – Revised (MET-R)** [12] evaluates the effect of executive function deficits on everyday functioning through a number of real-world tasks (e.g. purchasing specific items, collecting and writing down specific information, arriving at a stated location). Tasks are performed in a hospital or community setting within the constraints of specified rules. The participant is observed performing the test and the number and type of errors (e.g. rule breaks, omissions) are recorded.
- **The Behavioural Assessment of the Dysexecutive Syndrome (BADS)** [13] predicts everyday problems associated with a major area of cognitive deficit that can impede functional recovery and the ability to respond to rehabilitation programmes.

- **The Delis-Kaplan Executive Function System (D-KEFS)** [14] is a neuropsychological test used to measure a variety of executive functions in children and adults. It includes nine tests that were designed to stand alone.

As with all neuropsychological assessments, it is important to consider whether additional factors may be impacting upon performance (see Chapter 4 regarding Acquired Brain Injury for more information).

Adaptations and considerations

✓ Encourage people to break down larger tasks into smaller achievable chunks. Dividing workloads into smaller components and focusing on just one at a time can make a difference. Useful tools to structure this include using ladders or stairs as an analogy, breaking a task down one step at a time, with each step getting closer to the overall goal.

✓ Verbal (positive statements) and physical encouragement (sitting with them/partially doing a task alongside) can help an individual particularly when they experience self-criticism in respect of being/feeling unable to complete a task.

✓ Offer individuals regular breaks, even if this is just to stretch their legs, or get a glass of water. As a minimum, try breaking for 5 to 10 minutes every hour if possible.

✓ Using visual symbols, such as a 'now and next' boards, calendars and lists can help people to understand what is happening, when it will happen and in what order.

✓ Try using voice recordings or notes to remind people of upcoming appointments, events, and deadlines.

✓ Suggest organisational apps to help with managing anxiety and overload.

✓ Try colour-coding materials to clearly focus attention or differentiate between items or tasks.

✓ Identify other professionals who can provide support (e.g. support staff at school, or managers at work) and schedule regular check-ins with them so that they may assist the individual to manage their workload and prioritise tasks.

✓ Try to put in place a clear daily structure and routine for the person.

✓ Ensure expectations of behaviour and levels of co-operation are clearly understood and remembered (using some of the above).

✓ Individuals with executive functioning difficulties will often manage better where noise and levels of stimulation are kept to a minimum; try where possible to provide a calm environment.

✓ Humour can be a useful tool to help diffuse difficult situations or to distract from an escalating situation if this is considered appropriate and safe to do so.

Signposting

Due to the fact that executive dysfunction is not a recognised standalone diagnosis, there are limited support networks available in respect of assisting individuals who experience such difficulties. However, there are often suggestions and resources regarding executive functioning difficulties included within the support services for associated conditions (e.g. brain injury).

↟ **Headway** – the UK based charity offering support for individuals affected by brain injury, has a page specifically regarding executive functioning difficulties: https://www.headway.org.uk/about-brain-in jury/individuals/effects-of-brain-injury/executive-dysfunction/

Sal case example

Sal was a 24-year-old single parent of two children, who were five and eight years old. Sal identified as non-binary from around the age of 14 years old. Sal had left school at 16 years old and soon after had their first child. They had never held a job, and they looked after the children full time. They lived in a council flat and claimed universal credit.

Sal was under the attention of social services due to concerns about their ability to care for their children. The children were often noted to attend school hungry, unclean and in clothing inappropriate for the weather. The older child was presenting with behaviour difficulties within school, and the younger child had not achieved some of their expected milestones. Teachers at the school had raised a safeguarding concern; however, they also conveyed their sense that Sal loved their children and was not intentionally harming them. Because of this, the school had been unable to make sense of why these difficulties were presenting, as they had met with Sal on several occasions to discuss the issues, and Sal had always presented as very willing and open to discussing the problems and had tried to work with the school to improve the situation.

Professionals involved in the case had wondered whether Sal had a Learning Disability, or possibly autism. However, diagnostic assessment indicated that Sal did not have autism and they were cognitively functioning at an average level overall. However, Sal's processing speed and working memory were found to be relative areas of weakness for them.

As such, a comprehensive assessment of executive functioning was completed. This demonstrated that Sal had significant deficits in several areas of executive functioning. Sal struggled to initiate tasks and required consistent external cues to get started on tasks, such as getting the clothes washing done, or making dinner, and given that Sal was a single parent, there was no other adult around to support them. Sal's difficulties even extended to tasks that Sal wanted to do such as taking a relaxing bath or getting an early night. Sal also had difficulties with planning and organisation skills, meaning that complex tasks such as getting the children ready in the morning (a task which involves lots of smaller steps, often simultaneously when there is more than one child!) were often delayed and resulted in the children being late for school. Sal had difficulties considering environmental factors when making decisions, and consequently the children were often dressed in shorts and t-shirts, or not wearing coats when the weather was cold. Sal often relied upon snack foods (e.g. bags of crisps, piece of fruit) to feed the children, stating that they were '*not a Michelin star chef*' and it seemed that they were unable to follow recipes especially those comprising multiple steps. Sal reported that they and the children were often hungry, despite there being enough food in the house.

However, Sal had good emotional understanding and control and realised that the difficulties that they were experiencing were impacting upon the children. Sal clearly loved the children and was willing to work with social services to develop their executive functioning skills further, using external cues such as phone alarms. They also enlisted the support of their mother to help and scheduled regular check-ins with the school. Through the aforementioned process, Sal's newfound understanding that the difficulties that they were experiencing was due to impaired executive functioning validated their experience, reduced their previous stance of self-blame and associated internal critical dialogue, and meant that professionals had a clearer understanding of Sal's strengths and needs which allowed for a more suitably tailored plan to be put in place to support Sal and their children.

References

1. Cotrena, C., Damiani Branco, L., Ponsoni, A., Samame, C., Milman Shansis, F., & Paz Fonseca, R. (2020). Executive functions and memory in bipolar disorders I and II: New insights from meta-analytic results. *Acta Psychiatrica Scandinavica*, 141(2), 110–130. doi:10.1111/acps.13121.
2. Parola, A., Salvini, R., Gabbatore, I., Colle, L., Berardinelli, L., & Bosco, F. M. (2020). Pragmatics, theory of mind and executive functions in schizophrenia: Disentangling the puzzle using machine learning. *PLoS One*, 15(3). doi:10.1371/journal.pone.0229603.
3. Xie, R., Sun, X., Yang, L., & Guo, Y. (2020). Characteristic executive dysfunction for high-functioning autism sustained to adulthood. *Autism Research*, 13(12), 2102–2121. doi:10.1002/aur.2304.
4. Zhang, S. Y., Qiu, S. W., Pan, M. R., Zhao, M. J., Zhao, R. J., Liu, L., ... & Qian, Q. J. (2021). Adult ADHD, executive function, depressive/anxiety symptoms, and quality of life: A serial two-mediator model. *Journal of Affective Disorders*, 293, 97–108. doi:10.1016/j.jad.2021.06.020.
5. Walsh, K. W. (1985). *Understanding Brain Damage: A Primer of Neuropsychological Evaluation*. London: Longman.
6. Teuber, H. L. (1964). The Riddle of the Frontal Lobe Function in Man. In J. M. Warren and K. Akert (Eds.), *The Frontal Granular Cortex and Behavior* (pp. 410–458). New York: McGraw Hill.
7. George, M. S. & Gilbert, S. (2018). Mental Capacity Act (2005) assessments: Why everyone needs to know about the frontal lobe paradox. *The Neuropsychologist*, 5, 59–66. doi:10.53841/bpsneur.2018.1.5.59.
8. Copstick, S., Turnbull, L. B., Tibbles, J., Ashworth, S., Swanepoel, H. J., Kinch, J., & Moffitt, J. (2023). Developing an understanding of the Frontal Lobe Paradox through clinical group discussions. *The Neuropsychologist*, 1 (16), 40–45. doi:10.53841/bpsneur.2023.1.16.40.
9. Wilson, B. A., Alderman, N., Burgess, P. W., Emslie, H., & Evans, J. J. (1996). *Behavioural Assessment of the Dysexecutive Syndrome*. Bury St. Edmunds, UK: Harcourt Assessment.
10. Leslie, F. V. C., Foxe, D., Daveson, N., Flannagan, E., Hodges, J. R., & Piguet, O. (2016). FRONTIER Executive Screen: A brief executive battery to differentiate frontotemporal dementia and Alzheimer's disease. *Journal of Neurology, Neurosurgery and Psychiatry*, 87(8), 831–835. doi:10.1136/jnnp-2015-311917.
11. Llinàs-Reglà, J., Vilalta-Franch, J., López Pousa, S., Calvó-Perxas, L., Torrents Rodas, D., & Garre-Olmo, J. (2017). The Trail Making Test. *Assessment*, 24(2), 183–196. doi:10.1177/1073191115602552.
12. Morrison, T. M., Giles, G. M., Ryan, J. D., Baum, C. M., Dromerick, A. W., Polatajko, H. J., & Edwards, D. F. (2013). Multiple Errands Test–Revised (MET–R): A performance-based measure of executive function in people with mild cerebrovascular accident. *American Journal of Occupational Therapy*, 67, 460–468. doi:10.5014/ajot.2013.007880.

13. Wilson, B. A., Alderman, N., Burgess, P. W., Emslie, H., & Evans, J. J. (1996). *Behavioural Assessment of the Dysexecutive Syndrome.* Bury St. Edmunds, UK: Harcourt Assessment.
14. Delis, D. C., Kaplan E., & Kramer, J. H. (2001). *Delis Kaplan Executive Function System (D-KEFS).* San Antonio, TX: The Psychological Corporation.

7 Learning Disability

Lyn Shelton

CONSULTANT FORENSIC PSYCHOLOGIST

Introduction

There are approximately 1.3 million people with a Learning Disability (LD) in England, including over 950,000 adults aged 18 or over [1]. LD is a widely recognised term in the UK and is utilised in the Department of Health documentation. Whilst other terms, such as Intellectual Disability, are becoming more widely used internationally, the term LD will be used within this chapter due to being well understood by health and social care professionals within the UK.

In England, almost 68,000 children have a statement of special educational needs (SEN) or an education, health and care (EHC) plan; they are identified as having primary SEN associated with an LD. Of those 68,000 children, 26% are educated in mainstream schools. Boys are more commonly diagnosed with SEN/LD than girls. It is also known that children from deprived areas and/or those eligible for free school meals were more likely to have a SEN associated with an LD. There are higher rates of moderate and severe LD diagnosed amongst Romany Gypsy children and higher rates of diagnosis of profound LD amongst Pakistani and Bangladeshi children [2].

This chapter is divided into the following sections:

1 Background
2 Things to look out for
3 Screening assessments
4 Specialist assessment
5 Adaptations and considerations
6 Signposting
7 Case examples
8 References

DOI: 10.4324/9781003510659-7

Background

An LD is different from a learning difficulty (see Chapter 8 relating to learning difficulties), which is a reduced intellectual ability for a specific form of learning and includes conditions such as dyslexia (reading), dyspraxia (affecting physical co-ordination) and Attention Deficit Hyperactivity Disorder (ADHD). An individual living with an LD may also have one or more learning difficulties.

An LD can occur when brain development is affected before or during birth, or in early childhood [3]. There are multiple factors that can impact upon the development of the brain during these periods, such as maternal illness during pregnancy, oxygen deprivation during birth, development of abnormal genes, inherited LD passed through maternal and/or paternal genes, and illness or injury during early childhood (e.g. meningitis) [4]. However, it is important to highlight that there is no known single cause of LD.

LD affects the way a person understands information and how they communicate. They can have difficulty understanding new or complex information, learning new skills and coping independently. LD is an official diagnosis, where the individual must meet several specific criteria in order to receive the diagnosis. The criteria include:

- Onset prior to the age of 18
- Intellectual functioning assessed as a Full-Scale Intellectual Quotient below 70
- Impaired adaptive functioning [5]

Adaptive functioning is a term used to describe how an individual living with LD may adapt to their difficulties in everyday life in order to function [5]. The World Health Organisation's (WHO) International Classification of Functioning, Disability and Health [6, 7] describes adaptive functioning as the distinction between the individual's ability and performance. As such, an individual with adaptive functioning difficulties may not have had the opportunity to acquire important skills. The Diagnostical and Statistical Manual of mental disorders (DSM-5-TR; 2022) [8] uses the term 'intellectual developmental disorder' (F70-F79) and lists criteria for the severity of LD: Mild, Moderate, Severe, and Profound. The International Classification of Diseases 11th Revision (ICD-11) [9] codes LD within 'disorders of intellectual development' (6A00) and classifies the severity of LD as:

- **Mild** – approximate IQ range of 50 to 69. Likely to result in some difficulties in the acquisition and comprehension of complex language concepts and academic skills. Most people can manage basic self-care, domestic, and practical activities, and can live and work relatively independently, but may require appropriate support.
- **Moderate** – approximate IQ range of 35 to 49. Likely to have basic language and academic skills, but some will manage basic self-care, domestic, and practical activities. Most will need considerable and consistent support to live and work independently.
- **Severe** – approximate IQ range of 20 to 34. Have very limited language and academic skills and may also have motor impairments. Typically need daily support in a supervised environment for adequate care but may acquire basic self-care skills with intensive training.
- **Profound** – IQ under 20. Results in very limited communication skills and may have basic concrete skills. May have motor and sensory impairments and typically need daily support in a supervised environment for adequate care.

Whilst these classifications can have different meanings (such as in education provisions and health services), the use of specifiers for these diagnoses enables a fuller description of the individual's case, how it impacts upon them and what current symptoms they experience. In addition to diagnostic specifiers (such as age of onset or severity ratings), neurodevelopmental disorders may also include specifiers associated with a medical condition (e.g. seizure disorder), genetic condition (e.g. trisomy 21) or environmental factor (e.g. low birth weight).

Things to look out for

It is likely that signs or symptoms of an LD will be evident during childhood; these typically become apparent during infancy, but for some this may not be observable until the child reaches school age. Common markers include developmental delays in areas such as rolling, sitting, crawling, walking or talking, achieving these at a slower rate than their age-related peers. The child may also have difficulty socialising or communicating with others or take longer to process information during conversation and also therefore to respond. Difficulties with daily living activities such as personal care or dressing might also become visible.

When a child with LD reaches school age, they are likely to perform lower than average in assessments and may struggle to learn academically. Difficulties applying logic or with problem solving, as well as having poor memory or recall, may also become apparent. The child may also experience difficulties understanding consequences of behaviour and how their actions have led to those consequences.

As mentioned previously in this chapter, determining the cause of an LD can be difficult, and often the cause of LD remains unknown; however, there are a number of key factors that could lead to/contribute to the development of an LD.

Environmental factors

- exposure to toxic substances such as prenatal alcohol exposure or substance misuse
- nutritional deficiencies such as prenatal iodine deficiency
- brain radiation
- illness, such as meningitis or measles
- injury/trauma to the brain in early childhood
- the mother becoming ill in pregnancy, for example, experiencing rubella
- very premature birth (usually less than 33 weeks gestation) which could lead to hypoxemia [10]
- childhood neglect or lack of stimulation in early life

Genetic factors

- inherited condition such as Fragile X syndrome [11]
- abnormal chromosomes such as Down's syndrome (trisomy 21) [12] or Turner syndrome
- comorbid diagnoses such as autism or ADHD.

It is common for individuals living with an LD to have co-occurring diagnoses (occurs when a healthcare professional assumes that a patient's presentation is due to their disability or coexisting mental health condition rather than fully exploring the cause of the patient's symptoms); in the past this has led to an underestimation of the link between LD and co-occurring diagnoses [13]. Research indicates that someone living with an LD is four to five times more likely to experience poor mental health; and around 25% are at increased risk of schizophrenia, depression and ADHD, amongst other psychiatric problems [14, 15].

Given the aforementioned difficulties that can be experienced by those with an LD, it is not surprising that this group of individuals is at a greater risk of engaging in behaviour that challenges[1] than those without this diagnosis; this may be related to personal factors such as co-occurring conditions, poor mental health, it may be linked to the severity of LD, communication difficulties, sensory processing difficulties and physical health problems [16]. Environmental factors also increase the risk of a person living with an LD presenting with behaviour that challenges. For example, some care environments may provide reduced opportunity for the individual to engage in meaningful activity or social interaction; these environments may be crowded and unpredictable, with increased likelihood of under- or over-stimulation such as bright lights, extreme heat, strong smells, noise and low engagement from staff or frequent staff changes. Sadly, there have been examples where such environments have subjected people living with an LD to horrific abuse and neglect (Winterbourne View) [17]; Whorlton Hall [18].

Like anyone, individuals living with an LD have unique strengths as well as challenges. Common challenges include having difficulties solving problems that necessitates additional teaching support, and assistance to establish and maintain relationships and to find and maintain employment. They may also require support with daily functioning which may result in them being unable to live independently. There is also a high prevalence of suicidal ideation and self-harm in people with an LD [20, 21].

Screening assessments

There are minimal valid and reliable screening assessments to identify the potential presence of LD. For children, the Child and Adolescent Intellectual Disability Screening Questionnaire (CAIDS-Q) [22] has been found to have good psychometric qualities [23]. It is a seven-item screening tool to be used with children and young people aged 6–18 years; it is scored by giving yes/no answers to items related to literacy, current and previous support from clinical and educational services, friendships and basic functional skills.

For adults and children, aged 6–99 and 11 months, the Wechsler Abbreviated Scale of Intelligence, Second Edition (WASI-II) [24] provides a brief, reliable measure of cognitive ability in clinical, educational, and research settings. It is a quick measure of verbal, non-verbal and general cognitive ability with four subtests; it takes approximately 30 minutes to complete.

Specialist assessment

For the more formal diagnostic assessment, obtaining a detailed background of the person is essential [25]; there should be a focus on neurodevelopmental history. Due to potential errors in self-report, this information should be supplemented with formal documentation where possible; an informant or advocate being present can also help to gain valid and reliable information.

The formal diagnostic process should incorporate an assessment of both cognitive ability and adaptive functioning. For cognitive ability, the Wechsler Intelligence Scale for Children, 5th edition (WISC-V) [26] is a commonly used assessment of intellectual functioning with good psychometric properties that measures a child's intellectual ability and five cognitive domains that impact performance, suitable for ages 6–16 years and 11 months. It contains five primary index scores (verbal comprehension, visual spatial, fluid reasoning, working memory and processing speed), the Full Scale IQ (FSIQ), General Ability Index (GAI; an estimate of general intellectual ability that is less reliant on working memory and processing speed relative to the FSIQ), Cognitive Proficiency Index (CPI; an estimate of the efficiency with which cognitive information is processed in learning, problem solving, and higher order reasoning), as well as three ancillary index scores that can be obtained with the ten primary subtests. The ancillary index scores provide additional information for specific clinical situations:

- **Quantitative Reasoning Index (QRI):** An indicator of quantitative reasoning skills which assists in more accurately predicting reading and maths achievement scores, creativity, future academic success, and success in gifted programmes.
- **Auditory Working Memory Index (AWMI):** An indicator of a child's auditory working memory skills and the ability to resist proactive interference for a purer measure of auditory working memory that complements the WMI.
- **Nonverbal Index (NVI):** A global measure of intellectual ability that does not require any expressive responses. This score may be useful for children with a variety of language-related issues, including English language learners, deaf or hard-of-hearing, or suspected language disorder or autism.

The British Psychological Society's Guidance on the Assessment and Diagnosis of Intellectual Disabilities in Adulthood [5] states that wherever possible, only the most up-to-date versions assessments of intellectual ability should be used and they should fulfil all of the following:

- *'They should be designed for individual (not group) administration;*
- *they should have been constructed on the basis of the normal distribution of general intelligence, and standardised using a representative sample of adults from across the United Kingdom;*
- *they should possess psychometric properties (reliability and validity) that lie within the range of scientific acceptability;*
- *they should be based upon a multidimensional, hierarchical model of intelligence, producing not just an overall score but also related index or composite scores'.*

([5], pp. 16–17)

For adults (age 16 to 90 years and 11 months), the only test of intellectual functioning which meets all these criteria is the Wechsler Adult Intelligence Scale, 4th edition (WAIS-IV) [27]. WAIS-IV yields Full Scale IQ, GAI, CPI, Index Scores, and subtest-level scaled scores. The four Index Scores are Verbal Comprehension (VCI), Perceptual Reasoning (PRI), Working Memory (WMI), and Processing Speed (PSI). The WAIS-IV includes 10 core subtests and five supplementary subtests. The WAIS-V is due to be published in the UK in 2026; the updated version will include separate visual spatial and fluid reasoning indexes, a more comprehensive measurement of working memory, a new quantitative reasoning index, alongside ancillary index scores. The WAIS-V will also be more accessible, including Nonverbal Index for expressive issues, Nonmotor Index and Motor-Reduced Processing Speed Index for motor issues.

If an individual does not use English as their first language, does not have an adequate use of English, or is non-verbal, the Leiter International Performance Scale, Third Edition (Leiter-30) [28] may be considered as an alternative to the WAIS-IV. The Leiter-3 is a completely non-verbal test of intelligence, which is claimed to be culture-free. However, it has not been standardised in the UK and concerns have been raised about the accuracy and reliability of earlier versions of the scale, particularly in the lower ranges of ability [29]. A further alternative is the Ravens' IQ test [30], this is a nonverbal test that aims to measure an individual's intelligence and abstract reasoning. However, some researchers have argued that the test is not a true measure of intelligence, as it only assesses certain types of cognitive abilities and does not take into account other important factors such as creativity, emotional intelligence, and social skills.

The assessment of adaptive functioning is less clearly defined [31]; however, the most up-to-date assessments tend to include conceptual, social and practical skills domains. There are two available assessments which cover most of the relevant criteria; the Adaptive Behaviour Assessment System, Third Edition (ABAS-3) [32] and the Vineland Adaptive Behaviour Scales, Third Edition (Vineland-3) [33]; however, neither of these cover all criteria for the UK as both are based on a USA normative sample.

The ABAS-3 is an individually administered, norm-referenced measure that assesses adaptive behaviour and related skills for individuals from birth through to 89 years of age. Information on children may be provided by parents/carers and/or teachers; information on adults may be provided by significant others, care providers, supervisors, and/or the individual themselves. ABAS-3 scores help describe a person's general adaptive behaviour, as well as their functioning in 11 related adaptive skill areas: Communication, Community Use, Functional Academics, School/Home Living, Health and Safety, Leisure, Self-Care, Self-Direction, Social, and Work (for older adolescents and adults).

The Vineland-3 is an individually administered measure of adaptive behaviour that is widely used to assess individuals with intellectual, developmental, and other disabilities. This is based on an informant's perspective, such as a parent/carer or teacher. It is used to assess personal and social skills used by individuals up to 90 years old in daily situations. The adaptive behaviour domains include an individual's communication skills, daily living skills, socialisation, and motor skills.

The clinician may also assess an individual's adaptive functioning through observation of tasks or facilitating discussion around the client telling or showing the clinician how or why they do something/complete a task. Observations can also include observing an individual in the community, such as observing them on a shopping trip to the supermarket; the clinician can observe organisational skills and how the client follows their shopping list and the route they take around the supermarket. These approaches can feel less formal for the client and subsequently a greater depth of information may be obtained.

Over two million individuals in the UK are estimated to lack capacity to make decisions in one or more areas of their life; this may be due to mental ill health, LD, dementia, or physical illnesses that affect brain function (such as delirium or head injury) [34]. It is therefore important to consider whether the individual has capacity to engage in assessment, as defined by the Mental Capacity Act [35]. The MCA has five key principles:

- **Principle 1:** Capacity should always be assumed. A patient's diagnosis, behaviour, or appearance should not lead you to presume capacity is absent.
- **Principle 2:** A person's ability to make decisions must be optimised before concluding that capacity is absent. All practicable steps must be taken, such as giving sufficient time for assessments; repeating assessments if capacity is fluctuating; and, if relevant, using interpreters, sign language, or pictures.
- **Principle 3:** Patients are entitled to make unwise decisions. It is not the decision but the process by which it is reached that determines if capacity is absent.
- **Principle 4:** Decisions (and actions) made for people lacking capacity must be in their best interests.
- **Principle 5:** Such decisions must also be the least restrictive option(s) for their basic rights and freedoms [36].

Capacity assessments should always be completed in the individual's best interest; the individual being assessed should also be offered support from an advocate to ensure that their voice is heard. The MCA process both safeguards the individual as well as aiding the clinician to make decisions in the best interest of the individual.

Adaptations and considerations

When assessing an individual's intellectual ability, a number of factors need to be taken into consideration by the assessor such as the environment, the client's mental health, medication, fatigue, motivation, effort, language, culture, ethnicity, sensory and other impairments. Each of these factors can impact on the reliability and validity of the assessment. The higher prevalence factors are discussed in more detail below.

Environmental considerations might include that the surroundings are free from noise [37], are well lit and are ventilated to allow for a temperature that is comfortable for the individual. The WAIS-IV manual is particularly descriptive about the layout of seating for the assessor and the individual.

Individuals with an LD are twice as likely to also have a mental health condition [38]. There are four risk factors that can increase the likelihood of an individual living with an LD developing poor mental health: biology and genetics increasing vulnerability to mental health difficulties, higher number of negative life events (resulting in higher stress levels which increases the likelihood of mental illness [39]), impact of others' attitudes (increased psychological distress) [40] and access to fewer resources and coping skills (increased incidences of anxiety and depression) [41]. The individual's mental health presentation should considered prior to testing as this could potentially skew the validity of the results.

The use of prescribed medication and/or illegal substances can impact an individual's performance on any assessment of cognitive functioning [42]; this could result in an underestimation of their IQ and subsequently lead to misdiagnosis.

Communication is key regardless of whether an individual has an LD or not; to increase accessibility it is essential to identify and support the individual's communication needs. For example, it is helpful to speak clearly, without jargon. Some clinicians may use alternative forms of communication such as sign language, talking mats[2] or Makaton. Check the person's understanding by asking them to tell you what you have said in their own words. Use of an advocate or supporting adult can also be helpful. It is essential that assessors and anyone liaising with the individual has undertaken appropriate training to enhance their knowledge of LD, such as the Oliver McGowan training (LD awareness training), which is mandated under the Health and Care Act 2022 [43].

Signposting

- Living with an LD does not mean that an individual will not have a good quality of life, in fact, a number of individuals with LD lead positive and fulfilling lives; this is usually dependent on their level of need. Whilst some individuals require 24-hour care and support, others live alone or have families of their own. Access to education, employment and social activities is again dependent on the individual's support needs, but this can and should be facilitated in line with their wants and needs.

- If an individual is given an LD diagnosis, it is important that they are offered support and/or intervention. Some individuals living with an LD present with behaviour that challenges and may benefit from specific interventions [44]. Interventions are best identified following a functional analysis[3] so that the function of the client's presenting behaviour is identified [45]. The primary intervention would be psychosocial, whilst medication may be considered, this should be a last resort and only if psychological interventions have not resulted in positive outcomes. Psychosocial interventions can vary but should always be evidence-based; they may include social interventions, Cognitive Behavioural Therapy (CBT), mindfulness, positive behavioural support,[4] and communication-based interventions. Outside of direct work with the individual, physical and social environmental changes can support the individual with any behaviour that challenges and subsequently increase their quality of life.

- It is helpful if a collaborative support plan can be developed with the individual alongside input from those who support/care for the individual. This should be bespoke to the individual and include background information, the person's strengths, their communication preferences, triggers to behaviour that challenges and how best to support the individual, as well as national and local support/ informative groups which may benefit the individual. Some national examples may include Mind, Mencap, the British Institute of Learning Disabilities (BILD) and Hft (charity that supports people with learning disability to live independent lives).

- Professionals working with individuals living with an LD also have access to a range of resources. These can be accessed via the afore-mentioned resources, but also through (non-exhaustive) the *NHS Digital Health and Care of People With LD Report* (this explores health condition comparisons between the LD and general popula-tions); the *Learning from Lives and Deaths Review* (LeDeR) annual reports (which explore causes of death in the LD population) and the People With LD in England website (which provides national statistics, services and support available for individuals with an LD and their families/carers).

Tanya case examples

Tanya is a 32-year-old woman living in supported accommodation. She was diagnosed with an LD during her early childhood years, characterised by difficulties with cognitive processing, problem-sol-ving, and adaptive functioning. Tanya was born to a supportive family, though her parents noticed developmental delays in speech and motor skills by the age of two. By the age of four Tanya was formally diagnosed with a mild LD, which was confirmed through psychological assessments.

Tanya's LD is classified as mild, with an IQ of 55. She has always struggled with tasks that require higher cognitive functioning, such as complex problem-solving and abstract thinking. However, Tanya has a good understanding of everyday life skills, including personal hygiene, cooking, and basic household chores. She attended a special education school throughout her primary and secondary years, where she received tailored support in the form of one-on-one teaching and assistance with schoolwork. Despite the challenges, Tanya developed strong social relationships with peers and teachers, demonstrating kindness and an eagerness to participate in group activities.

Tanya left school at the age of 18 and, after a short period in a local day service, moved into supported accommodation. Here, she was provided with a team of support workers who assist her with daily tasks and help her navigate social and community settings. Over the years, Tanya has made significant progress in terms of independence and life skills, although she continues to face challenges.

Tanya currently resides in a small, shared house with two other residents, who themselves have varying levels of LD. Her accommodation is part of a local service that supports adults with LD to live as independently as possible, offering both social and personal care support. Tanya benefits from a structured daily routine, which includes assistance with managing finances, cooking meals, and participating in local community activities, such as attending a day centre for social interaction.

In terms of medical care, Tanya regularly attends appointments with her general practitioner (GP) for routine health checks and medication management. Tanya does not have any major physical health conditions but requires assistance in managing her emotional well-being, particularly with anxiety and occasional mood fluctuations.

Tanya is generally well-liked by her peers and enjoys attending social events, including local community gatherings and craft workshops. However, she sometimes struggles with communication and can find it difficult to assert herself in group settings. Tanya often relies on her support workers to act as intermediaries in these situations, helping her express her preferences or concerns. Although she has a few close friends, Tanya tends to form stronger relationships with support staff, as they provide her with a sense of security and guidance.

One of Tanya's significant challenges is her occasional difficulty in making decisions, particularly when faced with unfamiliar situations. For example, Tanya struggles to decide what to buy when she goes shopping or to choose an activity without assistance. She has a tendency to defer decision-making to others, which can limit her autonomy and cause her frustration.

Tanya's journey demonstrates the importance of providing structured, individualised support to adults with an LD. With the right support, Tanya has made considerable strides in living a more independent and fulfilling life, but she continues to face challenges in decision-making and social interactions. Her case highlights the ongoing need for tailored interventions that promote greater autonomy while ensuring a strong safety net through ongoing care and support.

Kye case examples

Kye is a 28-year-old man living independently in a one-bedroom flat in a suburban area of the UK. He has a diagnosis of mild LD, which was identified during early childhood after assessments showed difficulties in cognitive processing and adaptive functioning. Kye's LD affects his ability to understand complex information and make decisions that involve abstract thinking. However, he is highly motivated to live independently and has made significant progress in his personal development over the years, with support from various services.

Kye was raised in a supportive family environment. His parents were proactive in seeking additional educational support for him throughout his school years, ensuring that he had access to resources such as special education teachers and speech therapy. Kye attended a special education school, where he was provided with a tailored curriculum that focused on practical life skills and social development. He left school at 18 years of age and began attending a local day centre for young adults with learning disabilities, where he continued to build his social and practical skills.

Kye has a mild LD, with an IQ of 65, which affects his ability to process information quickly and solve problems independently. Despite these challenges, he has always been highly engaged in his education and determined to achieve his goals. In school, he excelled in subjects that required hands-on learning, such as art, music, and physical education, which contributed to his sense of accomplishment and self-esteem.

Kye received additional support after leaving school through a local learning disability service that provided guidance in managing daily living skills. He underwent regular assessments to monitor his progress and identify areas where further support was needed. At 22, Kye moved into independent living, initially with help from a support worker who helped him manage household tasks, finances, and social interactions. Over time, Kye has gained more confidence in living alone, and he now only requires occasional assistance with budgeting and decision-making.

Kye currently lives independently, managing his own flat with minimal external help. He has a structured daily routine, which includes meal preparation, cleaning, and grocery shopping. Kye is proud of his independence and enjoys taking care of his home. He has developed a strong sense of personal responsibility and is proactive in maintaining his living space, ensuring it is tidy and organised.

Kye works part-time in a local charity shop, where he helps with sorting donations, arranging items for display, and assisting customers. His work is fulfilling, and he enjoys interacting with people in the community. The role provides Kye with both a sense of purpose and the opportunity to develop work-related skills. Although Kye sometimes struggles with tasks that require multitasking or problem-solving under pressure, his employer is supportive and has made reasonable adjustments, including providing clear instructions and breaking tasks into manageable steps. Kye's work colleagues are also understanding, and he has built strong, supportive relationships with them.

Outside of work, Kye has a variety of hobbies that help him relax and stay active. He enjoys playing football with friends on the weekends and is part of a local amateur team. Kye also has an interest in painting and often spends his free time working on art projects at home. These activities give him a sense of accomplishment and allow him to express himself creatively.

Kye is a sociable person and values his friendships. He maintains close relationships with his family, often visiting them on weekends, and has a small circle of friends with whom he enjoys social activities. While Kye can struggle with managing his emotions in stressful situations, his friends and family are understanding and provide support when needed.

A key challenge for Kye is his difficulty with complex decision-making and long-term planning. He occasionally requires guidance when making important decisions, such as managing his finances or planning for future goals. Despite these challenges, Kye remains optimistic and is determined to continue leading an independent life.

Kye's case highlights the potential for individuals with an LD to live independently and lead fulfilling lives with the right support systems in place. His journey illustrates how structured routines, work opportunities, and supportive social networks can significantly enhance the quality of life for people with an LD. Although Kye faces certain challenges, his determination and the assistance he receives enable him to navigate life successfully, pursue his hobbies, and contribute meaningfully to his community.

Notes

1 Challenging behaviour is commonly defined as 'culturally abnormal behaviour (s) of such intensity, frequency or duration that the physical safety of the person or others is likely to be placed in serious jeopardy, or behaviour which is likely seriously limit use of, or result in the person being denied access to ordinary community facilities' (p. 4) [19].
2 A Talking Mat is a visual communication tool that helps people who may have communication difficulties, such as those with learning disabilities, to share their thoughts and feelings.
3 Functional analysis is a method used to examine the causes and consequences of a specific behaviour. It is typically used with individuals with learning disabilities to examine how they might be communicating their unmet needs through their behaviour.
4 **Positive behavioural support** (PBS) is a person centred framework for providing long-term **support** to people with a learning disability, and/or autism, including those with mental health conditions, who have, or may be at risk of developing, **behaviours** that challenge. The overall aim of PBS is to improve the quality of a person's life and that of the people around them.

References

1. Public Health England (2023). *Learning disability: Applying all our health.* London: PHE.
2. Public Health England (2020). *People with learning disabilities in England.* London: PHE.
3. Fraser, D. M. & Cooper, M. A. (2009). *Myles textbook for midwives: The world's favourite midwifery textbook!.* London: Churchill Livingstone.
4. Sadler, T. W. (2010). Urogenital system. In: *Langman's medical embryology.* Philadelphia, PA: Walters Kluwer.
5. British Psychological Society (BPS). (2015). Guidance on the assessment and diagnosis of intellectual disabilities in adulthood. Retrieved from www.bps.org.uk.

6. World Health Organization. (2001). *International classification of functioning, disability, and health.* Geneva: Author.
7. World Health Organization. (2007). *International classification of functioning, disability, and health: Children and youth version.* Geneva: Author.
8. American Psychiatric Association. (2022). *Diagnostic and statistical manual of mental disorders fifth edition – text revision (DSM-5-TR®).* American Psychiatric Association.
9. World Health Organization. (2022). *International classification of diseases, 11th Revision (ICD-11).* Geneva: Author.
10. Gustafsson, C. (2003). Intellectual disability and mental health problems: Evaluation of two clinical assessment instruments, occurrence of mental health problems and psychiatric care utilisation (Doctoral dissertation, Acta Universitatis Upsaliensis).
11. Coffee, B., Keith, K., Albizua, I., Malone, T., Mowrey, J., Sherman, S. L. & Warren, S. T. (2009). Incidence of fragile X syndrome by newborn screening for methylated FMR1 DNA. *The American Journal of Human Genetics,* 85(4), 503–514. doi:10.1016/j.ajhg.2009.09.007.
12. Parker, S. E., Mai, C. T., Canfield, M. A., Rickard, R., Wang, Y., Meyer, R. E., Anderson, P., Mason, C. A., Collins, J. S., Kirby, R. S. & Correa, A. (2010). Updated National Birth Defects Prevention Network. (2010). Updated national birth prevalence estimates for selected birth defects in the United States, 2004–2006. *Birth Defects Research Part A: Clinical and Molecular Teratology,* 88(12), 1008–1016. doi:10.1002/bdra.20735.
13. American Psychiatric Association. (2013). *Diagnostic and statistical manual of mental disorders.* (DSM-5®). American Psychiatric Pub.
14. Bouras, N. (Ed.). (1999). *Psychiatric and behavioural disorders in developmental disabilities and mental retardation.* Cambridge University Press.
15. Fletcher, R., Loschen, E., Stavrakaki, C. & First, M. (2007). DM-ID: diagnostic manual – intellectual disability: A textbook of diagnosis of mental disorders in persons with intellectual disability. *Journal of Mental Health Research in Intellectual Disabilities,* 29. doi:10.1176/appi.ps.59.6.699-a.
16. NICE (2015). Challenging behaviour and learning disabilities: Prevention and interventions for people with learning disabilities whose behaviour challenges. National Institute of Health and Care Excellence. http://www.nice.org.uk.
17. Flynn, M. (2012). *Winterbourne View Hospital. A serious case review.* Gloucestershire, UK: South Gloucestershire Council.
18. Willis, D. (2020). Whorlton Hall, Winterbourne View and Ely Hospital: Learning from failures of care. *Learning Disability Practice,* 23(6). doi:10.7748/ldp.2020.e2049.
19. Emerson, E. (1995). *Challenging behaviour: Analysis and intervention in people with learning disabilities.* Cambridge: Cambridge University Press.
20. Merrick, J., Merrick, E., Lunsky, Y. & Kandel, I. (2005). Suicide behavior in persons with intellectual disability. *The Scientific World Journal,* 5, 729–735. doi:10.1100/tsw.2005.91.

21. Dodd, P., Doherty, A. & Guerin, S. (2016). A systematic review of suicidality in people with intellectual disabilities. *Harvard Review of Psychiatry*, 24 (3), 202–213. doi:10.1097/HRP.0000000000000095.

22. McKenzie, K., Paxton, D., Murray, G.C., Milanesi, P. & Murray, A. L. (2012). The evaluation of a screening tool for children with an intellectual disability: The Child and Adolescent Intellectual Disability Screening Questionnaire. *Research in Developmental Disabilities*, 33, 1068–1075. doi:10.1016/j.ridd.2012.01.015.

23. McKenzie, K., Murray, G., Murray, A., Delahunty, L., Hutton, L., Murray, K. & O'hare, A. (2019). Child and Adolescent Intellectual Disability Screening Questionnaire to identify children with intellectual disability. *Developmental Medicine & Child Neurology*, 61(4), 444–450. doi:10.1111/dmcn.13998.

24. Wechsler, D. (2011). *Wechsler Abbreviated Scale of Intelligence (WASI-II)*, 2nd ed. APA Psychological Tests.

25. Spreen, O. & Strauss, E. (1998). *A compendium of neuropsychological tests*, 2nd ed. Oxford: Oxford University Press.

26. Wechsler, D. (2014). *WISC-V: Technical and interpretive manual*. Research study. Bloomington, MN: Pearson.

27. Wechsler, D. (2008). *Wechsler Adult Intelligence Scale: Fourth edition administration and scoring manual*. San Antonio, TX: Pearson.

28. Roid, G. H., Miller, L. J., Pomplun, M. & Koch, C. (2013). *Leiter International Performance Scale – Third edition (Leiter-3)*. Wood Dale, IL: Stoelting Co.

29. Glenn, S. & Cunningham, C. C. (2005). Performance of young people with Down's Syndrome on the Leiter-R and the British Picture Vocabulary Scales. *Journal of Intellectual Disability Research*, 48, 239–244. doi:10.1111/j.1365–2788.2005.00643.x.

30. Raven, J. & Raven, J. (2003). Raven progressive matrices. In R. S. McCallum (Ed.), *Handbook of nonverbal assessment* (pp. 223–237). Kluwer Academic/Plenum Publishers.

31. Avery, G. & Sullivan, F. (2013). Use of the Vineland Adaptive Behaviour Scales (2nd ed.) in the assessment of adults with intellectual disabilities: Clinical observations. *Clinical Psychology Forum*, 246, 13–17.

32. Harrison, P. L. & Oakland, T. (2015). *ABAS-3*. Torrance: Western Psychological Services.

33. Pepperdine, C. R. & McCrimmon, A. W. (2018). *Test review: Vineland Adaptive Behavior Scales, (Vineland-3) by Sparrow, SS, Cicchetti, DV, & Saulnier, CA*. Pearson Assessments US.

34. NICE (2018). Decision making and capacity: NG108. National Institute of Health and Care Excellence. http://www.nice.org.uk.

35. Mental Capacity Act 2005. Available at: www.legislation.gov.uk/ukpga/2005.

36. Nicholson, T. R., Cutter, W. & Hotopf, M. (2008). Assessing mental capacity: The mental capacity act. *BMJ*, 336(7639), 322–325. doi:10.1136/bmj.39457.485347.80.

37. Klatte, M., Wegner, M. & Hellbrück, J. (2005). *Noise in the school environment and cognitive performance in elementary school children. Part B-Cognitive psychological studies.* In Forum Acusticum2005.

38. Emerson, E. & Hatton, C. (2007). Mental health of children and adolescents with intellectual disabilities in Britain. *The British Journal of Psychiatry*, 191 (6), 493–499. doi:10.1192/bjp.bp.107.038729.

39. Bond, L., Carroll, R., Mulryan, N., O'Dwyer, M., O'Connell, J., Monaghan, R. ... & McCarron, M. (2019). The association of life events and mental ill health in older adults with intellectual disability: Results of the wave 3 intellectual disability supplement to the Irish longitudinal study on ageing. *Journal of Intellectual Disability Research*, 63(5), 454–465. doi:10.1111/jir.12595.

40. Pelleboer-Gunnink, H. A., Van Oorsouw, W. M., van Weeghel, J. & Embregts, P. J. (2021). Stigma research in the field of intellectual disabilities: A scoping review on the perspective of care providers. *International Journal of Developmental Disabilities*, 67(3), 168–187. doi:10.1080/20473869.2019.1616990.

41. Austin, K. L., Hunter, M., Gallagher, E. & Campbell, L. E. (2018). Depression and anxiety symptoms during the transition to early adulthood for people with intellectual disabilities. *Journal of Intellectual Disability Research*, 62(5), 407–421. doi:10.1111/jir.12478.

42. Powell, J. (2004). The effects of medication and other substances on cognitive functioning. In: *Clinical neuropsychology: A practical guide to assessment and management for clinicians* (p. 99). Chichester: Wiley-Blackwell.

43. Health and Care Act 2022.

44. Ali, A., Blickwedel, J. & Hassiotis, A. (2014). Interventions for challenging behaviour in intellectual disability. *Advances in Psychiatric Treatment*, 20(3), 184–192. doi:10.1192/apt.bp.113.011577.

45. O'Neill, R., Horner, R., Albin, R., Sprague, J., Storey, K. & Newton, J. (1997). *Functional assessment and program development for problem behaviour: A practical handbook.* Melbourne: Brooks Cole Publishing.

8 Specific Learning Differences

Jessica Newcombe

SPECIAL EDUCATIONAL NEEDS ASSISTANT HEADTEACHER

Introduction

A note on language: In empirical research and in practice in England, dyslexia, dyspraxia, dysgraphia, and dyscalculia are commonly discussed as a collective and referred to as Specific Learning Difficulties (and are referred to as Specific Learning Disorders in the DSM-5-TR; 2022). A neuro-affirmative approach advocates instead for use of the term 'Specific Learning Differences' to signify that it is a different way of thinking rather than related to intelligence. Throughout this chapter, the term **Specific Learning Difference(s) (SpLD)** will be used.

Additionally, identity-first language will be used throughout. For example, someone who is dyslexic does not have or live with dyslexia, they are dyslexic.

Dyslexia, dysgraphia and dyscalculia are terms commonly used by professionals in the UK; however, within the latest diagnostic manuals such as DSM-5-TR [1], these are diagnosed as Specific Learning Disorder (SLD) with impairment in reading, writing or mathematics. Similarly in the ICD-11 [2], dyslexia, dysgraphia and dyscalculia are diagnosed under the umbrella of Developmental Learning Disorder (DLD) with impairment in reading, writing, expression or mathematics.

The terms SLD and DLD as set out in the DSM-5-TR and ICD-11, are characterised by learning disorders that use academic skills; these umbrella terms are broken down into sub-categories:

- **Reading (dyslexia)** difficulties with word recognition, reading fluency and decoding words

DOI: 10.4324/9781003510659-8

- **Writing (dysgraphia)** challenges with spelling, grammar, punctuation and organising written work
- **Mathematics (dyscalculia)** problems with number sense, memorising facts and performing calculations

These three profiles are known to frequently co-occur.

Dyspraxia is a term used in the UK that does not fall under the umbrella category of SLD, in the DSM-5-TR, rather this is referred to as a 'Developmental Coordination Disorder (DCD)'. Within the ICD-11 this is diagnosed under the term 'Developmental Motor Coordination Disorder'. These profiles encompass motor performance that is substantially below expected levels.

Table 8.1 below provides details about each domain as it is represented in the DSM-5-TR and ICD-11.

Note: The language in this chapter will use the commonly used terms in the UK, dyslexia, dyspraxia, dysgraphia and dyscalculia which, as stated, all fall under the umbrella term as SpLD. Whilst the terms SLD and DLD are medical terms and used for clinical diagnosis, the term SpLD is often preferred, especially when speaking with or about children as it prevents the child being labelled as 'disordered'.

This chapter will highlight the process of getting a diagnosis, the current attitudes, the approaches adopted in the English education system, and the support networks available in England. This chapter explores each domain of SpLD and the potential impact that these may have on a person's life.

The majority of the information in this chapter is derived from an English perspective (hence why the terms dyslexia, dyspraxia, dyscalculia and dysgraphia are used). This means that unless otherwise stated information relating to SpLD comes from empirical research, legislation, and governing bodies based in England. There are of course inherent difficulties with this Anglocentric[1] view of SpLD which shall be addressed later in this chapter.

Despite there being different specifiers for each SpLD domain there are several commonly impacted functions between the conditions, these include, **attention, organisation, working memory, time management, listening skills, sensory perception**, and **speed of processing**. SpLD are often hidden (i.e. people will look and behave just like their peers and may even demonstrate no immediate learning differences). SpLDs can co-occur and are lifelong conditions [3].

Table 8.1 Key characteristics of each domain of SpLD

Domain	What it looks like	Diagnostic and Statistical Manual of Mental Disorder 5th Edition Text Revision (DSM-5-TR, 2022) [1]	International Classification of Diseases 11th Revision (ICD-11, 2024)
Dyslexia	A pattern of learning differences characterised by challenges with accurate or fluent word recognition and requiring support with decoding and spelling.	Referred to as an 'impairment with reading' and includes word reading accuracy, reading rate or fluency, and reading comprehension. Persistently inaccurate or slow and effortful reading (e.g., reads single words aloud incorrectly or slowly and hesitantly, often guessing words). Difficulty understanding the meaning of what is read (e.g., may read text accurately but not understand the sequence, relationships, inferences, or deeper meaning).	Referred to as an 'impairment with reading' and includes word reading accuracy, reading fluency, and reading comprehension. The individual's performance in reading is markedly below what would be expected for chronological age and level of intellectual functioning and results in significant impairment in the individual's academic or occupational functioning.
Dysgraphia	Challenges related to writing.	Referred to as an 'impairment in written expression' and includes spelling accuracy, grammar and punctuation accuracy, and clarity or organization of written expression. Persistent difficulties with spelling (e.g., may add, omit, or substitute vowels or consonants). Difficulties with written expression (e.g., makes multiple grammatical or punctuation errors, lacks clarity, poor paragraph organization, or excessively poor handwriting).	Referred to as an 'impairment in written expression' and includes spelling accuracy, grammar and punctuation accuracy, and organisation and coherence of ideas in writing. The individual's performance in written expression is markedly below what would be expected for chronological age and level of intellectual functioning and results in significant impairment in the individual's academic or occupational functioning.

Domain	What it looks like	Diagnostic and Statistical Manual of Mental Disorder 5th Edition Text Revision (DSM-5-TR, 2022) [1]	International Classification of Diseases 11th Revision (ICD-11, 2024)
Dyscalculia	Challenges with numbers and arithmetic.	Referred to as an 'impairment in mathematics' and includes number sense, memorisation of arithmetic facts, accurate or fluent calculation, and accurate mathematical reasoning. Challenges with processing mathematical information, learning arithmetic and performing mathematic calculations which persist even when there are no other influential factors such as adequate social-economical and cultural opportunities and in a setting that provides an acceptable standard of education in maths [1]. Persistent difficulties mastering number sense, number facts, or calculation (e.g., poor understanding of numbers, their magnitude, and relationships; counts on fingers to add single-digit numbers instead of recalling math facts). Difficulties with mathematical reasoning (e.g., severe difficulty applying mathematical concepts, facts, or procedures to solve quantitative problems).	Referred to as an 'impairment in mathematics' and includes number sense, memorisation of number facts, accurate calculation, fluent calculation, and accurate mathematic reasoning. The individual's performance in mathematics or arithmetic is markedly below what would be expected for chronological or developmental age and level of intellectual functioning and results in significant impairment in the individual's academic or occupational functioning.

Domain	What it looks like	Diagnostic and Statistical Manual of Mental Disorder 5th Edition Text Revision (DSM-5-TR, 2022) [1]	International Classification of Diseases 11th Revision (ICD-11, 2024)
Dyspraxia	Affects gross and fine motor skills and physical coordination and can often affect handwriting.	Children whose motor coordination is less than expected for chronologic age and intelligence. It is not due to an identifiable medical disorder, and the coordination differences interfere with daily activities or academic achievement [2].	Developmental motor coordination disorder is characterised by a significant delay in the acquisition of gross and fine motor skills and impairment in the execution of coordinated motor skills that manifest in clumsiness, slowness, or inaccuracy of motor performance. Co-ordinated motor skills are substantially below that expected given the individual's chronological age and level of intellectual functioning. Onset of coordinated motor skills difficulties occurs during the developmental period and is typically apparent from early childhood. Coordinated motor skills difficulties cause significant and persistent limitations in functioning (e.g., in activities of daily living, schoolwork, and vocational and leisure activities).

This chapter is divided into the following sections:

1   Background
2   Heterogeneity within specific learning differences
3   Things to look out for
4   Screening assessment
5   Specialist assessment
6   Adaptations and considerations
7   Signposting
8   Case examples
9   References

The most commonly occurring domain of SpLD is 'impairment with reading' (referred to by the most commonly used term of 'dyslexia' throughout this chapter) and as such it has been the focus of most empirical investigations, this is reflected in the current chapter with greater focus given to dyslexia.

Background

Below is a chronology of the key events leading to the current understanding of each domain of SpLD.

Dyslexia

There are myriad symptoms that dyslexic people experience; it is often assumed that dyslexics only struggle to read, however having dyslexia presents differences that are unique for each person. Dyslexia is far more than simply a difficulty with reading, and it is important that people do not automatically assume that all reading difficulties are due to dyslexia [4].

The most influential current description of dyslexia is that of the UK's Rose Review [5], formed to recommend best practices in identifying and teaching children with dyslexia and literacy difficulties. In the Rose Review, dyslexia is defined as:

> A learning difficulty that primarily affects the skills involved in accurate and fluent word reading and spelling. Characteristic features of dyslexia are difficulties in phonological awareness, verbal memory and verbal processing speed. Dyslexia occurs across the range of intellectual abilities [5].

Table 8.2 Chronology of key events related to dyslexia [6]

Timeline	Key Events
1877	**Adolph Kussmaul** termed the phrase 'word blindness' and believed it was related to an ocular (eye) deficit.
1887	**Rudolph Berlin** coined the term 'dyslexia', which brought the phrase in line with other common diagnoses such as alexia (the inability to recognize or read written words or letters).
1920s	**Dr Samuel Torrey Orton** defined dyslexia as 'cross lateralisation of the brain'.
1960s–1970s	Influential texts on dyslexia emerged and identified 'developmental dyslexia' as an issue requiring urgent official attention. *The Dyslexic Child* (1970) [7]. 1972: Tizard Committee's Report: *Children with Specific Reading Difficulties* [8]. 1978 Warnock Report: Report of the Committee of Enquiry into the Education of Handicapped Children and Young People [9].
1987	The government stated the importance of the early identification of dyslexia to ensure the correct intervention could be delivered.
2009	The Rose Review [5] argued that dyslexia was not only impactful upon reading but also that it affected spelling, word fluency, phonological awareness, and memory.
2013	A change in the terminology with the removal of dyslexia, in the DSM-5 (2013); instead the term Specific Learning Disorder is used to describe difficulties with reading, difficulties with word recognition, reading fluency and decoding words. The addition of the umbrella term SLD to encompass three learning disorders (reading, mathematics, and written expression) into one overarching diagnosis.
Today (2024)	Today's understanding of dyslexia includes personal accounts of symptoms, and experiences that describe the challenges people face with learning and their day-to-day life. With this knowledge the awareness of how dyslexia affects each person individually has been accumulated to discover the impacts on peoples' lives [4].

Dyscalculia

Dyscalculia is distinct from more generalised maths difficulties or math anxiety. The following definition of dyscalculia was developed by the British Dyslexia Association Dyscalculia Committee and was accepted by the SpLD Assessment Standards Committee (SASC) who regulated assessment in 2019.

Mathematics difficulties are best thought of as a continuum, not a distinct category, and they have many causal factors. Dyscalculia falls at

Table 8.3 Chronology of key events related to dyspraxia

Timeline	Key events
1920s–1940s	**Dr Samuel Orton's research** recognised the symptoms of dyspraxia as a SpLD. Orton utilised the term clumsiness.
1972	The Clumsy Child [10] was published. 'Clumsiness' is a term still associated with dyspraxia today.
1980s	The term dyspraxia was used for the first time in 1989; the term clumsy child was discontinued.
1987	Diagnostic and Statistical Manual of Mental Disorder DSM-IV provided a diagnosis for DCD (known as dyspraxia in the UK).
2010	Dyspraxia UK was founded.

one end of the spectrum and will be distinguishable from other maths issues due to the severity of difficulties with number sense, including subitising, symbolic and non-symbolic magnitude comparison, and ordering. It can occur singly but often co-occurs with other specific learning difficulties, mathematics anxiety and medical conditions.

[7]

Dyspraxia

The historical journey of dyspraxia began in the mid-nineteenth century and was used to describe the lack of ability to execute or carry out skilled movements and gestures, despite having the physical ability and desire to perform them.

Heterogeneity within specific learning differences

Age

Individuals who receive a late diagnosis often do so when they attend university, as the nuances in their way of thinking and their learning style become more apparent when the educational demands change, for example, essay writing and note taking. Difficulties with note taking and essay writing are often associated with differences in working memory.

The difficulties that a person might experience associated with dyspraxia can change over time, depending on their environment, responsibilities, and the daily life challenges that they face. As such, a person's condition may not be identified until they are an adult.

Sex and gender

Dyslexia is related to differences in the way the brain processes language and is not specifically related to gender; however, boys may be more likely to receive a dyslexia diagnosis associated with them receiving less reading instruction than girls.

Dyslexic girls may present differently from boys and have different cognitive profiles. For instance, girls may be more likely to develop compensatory mechanisms, such as relying on phonological processing,[2] memorisation or context clues, which can mask their difficulties and make diagnosis more challenging than for dyslexic boys. This can contribute to the underdiagnosis or misdiagnosis of dyslexia in girls.

Dyspraxic girls are more likely to mask and conceal their difficulties, especially in childhood, and females often receive a diagnosis later in life compared to males [12]. Society often expects boys to be more interested in sports, often making differences more noticeable at a younger age for males. Additionally, dyspraxia often co-occurs against male-dominated diagnoses such as Attention Deficit Hyperactivity Disorder (ADHD), dyslexia and autism, such that dyspraxia might be picked up as an additional or unexpected diagnosis.

Social economic status, race and ethnicity

Working-class families are less likely to have access to a dyslexia assessment as identified difficulties with literacy may be assumed to be associated with socio-economic factors. Working-class families are less likely to have the means or the knowledge regarding how to source a dyslexia diagnosis [12]. Race and dyslexia in the UK are under-researched; in the US, assumptions surrounding race inform beliefs about academic potential. For example, learning difficulties are more commonly expected and dyslexia less likely to be considered for Black individuals [13].

There is some controversy surrounding dyslexia identification and it is sometimes referred to as a 'middle-class myth'. This train of thought suggests that those people with greater social capital and psychological awareness (middle-class families) are more likely to seek, obtain and be able to afford an assessment. Dyslexia assessments rely on profiling and there are differences with the interpretation of the assessments. Some people wish to focus on intervention rather than identification, as the same adaptations and strategies can be useful for those with or without a diagnosis. However, resources are often reserved for those who have a diagnosis (given limited budgets and resources) hence some families are keen to push for a diagnosis, as it enables different adaptations to be accessed for those who may be struggling with literacy skills and reading [14].

(⊠)   **Things to look out for**

Table 8.4 Common examples of how SpLD affects how people process and
       learn information

Characteristic	What you might see
⚲ Curiosity and hyperactivity	This may present as being easily distractable with shifts in attention. Losing train of thought easily during a conversation.
⚲ Clumsiness and spatially unaware	This may present as 'bumping' into items and people, misjudging spatial gaps when navigating furniture in rooms. Discoordination in sports, games and everyday life such as tripping over when walking.
⚲ Difficulties in phonological awareness	Not recognising rhyming words and / or mispronouncing words
⚲ Poor verbal memory and verbal processing speed	Lack of word accuracy when reading
⚲ Short-term memory issues	Being forgetful when someone has just been told something, for example, being given instructions and immediately forgetting them
⚲ A high level of curiosity and wide attention span of the environment	Being highly aware of the environment, noticing everything and constantly scanning the surroundings. This can often be mistaken for attention deficit disorder (ADD) [12].
⚲ Being highly intuitive and insightful	Being able to read people's emotions and respond with empathy
⚲ Making lots of careless mistakes such as with reading and with coordination (handwriting)	Lots of mistakes with written work, such as typos, grammar, spelling mistakes, jumbled and unorganised thoughts
⚲ Being articulate with good verbal language	A good communicator and articulate person, who can verbally explain their thoughts, ideas and arguments
⚲ Difficulties listening	When listening, appearing uninterested as though daydreaming, lost in their own thoughts or distracted
⚲ Difficulties with sequencing (completing things in the correct order)	Jumbled thoughts and being disorganised when preparing for events such as leaving the house and getting ready for school or work

Screening assessment

Children in the UK are not routinely screened in school for SpLD, but many schools use screening tests to guide the development of school support for children who are experiencing literacy difficulties. Screening tests can help to identify those who may need intervention or support or may benefit from a full diagnostic assessment.

Dysgraphia

Suspected dysgraphia can be screened through online checklists and questionnaires; these are not official and give an indication as to whether dysgraphia is present, examples include:

- https://www.esc15.net/cms/lib/TX50000034/Centricity/Domain/28/Dysgraphia%20Assessment%20outline.pdf
- https://specialneedsresourceblog.com/wp-content/uploads/2019/08/dysgraphia-checklist.pdf
- Dysgraphia Test & Online Screener for Children – Lexercise

Dyscalculia

Suspected dyscalculia can be screened through online checklists and questionnaires; however, these are not official and give an indication of whether or not dyscalculia is probable. These checklists and online questions are not clinical and are designed to guide a person to decide whether a diagnosis warrants pursuing. Some examples include:

- https://www.dyscalculia.me.uk/Freedyscalculiatest.pdf
- https://uk.smartickmethod.com/pdfs/dyscalculia/Dyscalculia_test_en.pdf
- https://view.officeapps.live.com/op/view.aspx?src=https%3A%2F%2Fwww.stevechinn.co.uk%2Fassets%2Ffiles%2FChecklist-for-Dyscalculia.categories.docx&wdOrigin=BROWSELINK
- https://discovery.ucl.ac.uk/id/eprint/10158637/7/ADD%20UP%20UCL%20Dyscalculia%20screeners%20and%20checklists.pdf

Specialist assessment

The DSM-5-TR (2022) sets out three different severity levels associated with a SpLD diagnosis based on the support that is likely to be required, these are:

- **Mild**: Some difficulties in one or two academic domains but can compensate or function well with support.
- **Moderate**: Marked difficulties in one or more academic domains, requiring specialised teaching or accommodations.
- **Severe**: Severe difficulties affecting several academic domains, requiring ongoing intensive individualised instruction and support services.

Dyslexia

Many personal accounts (e.g. within the literature and on social media) about receiving a dyslexia diagnosis describe it as having been life-changing, associated with it having helped the person understand their life-long difficulties with learning. This, in turn, can lead people to experience increased self-esteem, feelings of relief and the realisation that they are able to learn, and are 'not stupid', which can be a common belief of dyslexic people [4].

In the UK, dyslexia can only be formally diagnosed through a diagnostic assessment carried out by a certified assessor, such as a psychologist specialising in specific learning difficulties (SpLD) registered with the Health Care Practitioners Council (HCPC), Specialist teacher/assessor with AMBDA and/or an Assessment Practising Certificate (APC).[3]

A diagnostic dyslexia assessment provides a clearer picture of the person's strengths and limitations as well as their cognitive profile. The diagnostic assessment is followed by a written report that provides details of the individual's dyslexic profile (if dyslexia is confirmed), signposting to other organisations or recommendations for further assessment of additional specific learning difficulties (if required) as well as recommendations regarding how to support the individual in the context of their study and/or day-to-day life.

A diagnostic assessment usually involves taking a detailed life history and administering a range of tests. The tests are designed to measure four areas: verbal reasoning, visual reasoning, working memory and processing speed, providing a profile of cognitive function. Generally, there is little variation in the performance across each of the four areas of ability for a neurotypical person (someone without a learning difference). Where dyslexia is present, an individual will typically perform better on tests of verbal and visual ability than on those assessing working memory and processing speed. The series of tests used internationally by psychologists to measure these four sets of abilities is known as the WAIS-IV (Wechsler Adult Intelligence Scale 4th edition); and for children below the age of 16 years, it is the WISC (Wechsler Intelligence Scale for children which is in its fifth edition).[4]

These tests examine:

- Reading and writing abilities
- Language development and vocabulary
- Logical reasoning
- Memory
- The speed an individual can process visual and auditory (sound) information
- Organisational skills
- Approaches to learning

Generally, the greater the discrepancy (the higher the peaks and lower troughs creating a spikey profile) the greater the severity of the specific learning difference.

Additional important factors that are considered during assessment include:

- General state of health
- Performance of certain tasks
- What the person being assessed would like to change or to happen

The assessment is aimed at gaining a clinical understanding of the challenges and frustrations that the person may be experiencing. It considers context, for example, do any identified differences present across settings (e.g. home, school, work) or are the challenges specific to one area. It also provides a narrative of the person's experience, which is triangulated with the other gathered data.

Dyspraxia

Assessment performance is scored and compared with age-related norms. For a diagnosis of dyspraxia, the following criteria must be met:

- Motor skills are significantly below the age-expected level taking into account the individual's opportunities to learn and use the skills.
- The lack of motor skills significantly and persistently affects the person's day-to-day activities and achievements.
- The symptoms first developed during an early stage of development. It is unusual for a diagnosis to be given before the age of 5 years.
- The lack of motor skills cannot be better explained by long-term delay in all areas (general Learning Disability) or by a rare medical condition [12].

Dyscalculia

The BDA (British Dyslexia Association) recommends that a formal diagnostic assessment should only be carried out by an assessor who is qualified to a level 7 in the assessment of dyscalculia and has AMBDA dyscalculia. A level 7 qualification in the assessment of dyslexia is not considered by the BDA to be sufficient. The BDA have appropriately trained assessors; please see details of the Dyscalculia Referral Assessment Service.[5]

Dysgraphia

Dysgraphia is assessed by evaluating motor, sensory, perceptual and cognitive functions via a battery of assessments. This can include the following:

- DASH 17 – Detailed assessment of speed of handwriting measures; precision skills, fine motor skills, speed alteration and symbol production.
- Beery VMI – Beery-Buktenica developmental test of visual–motor integration measures the integration of motor and visual skills, motor co-ordination and visual perception.
- WAIS-IV – Wechsler adult intelligence scale can measure, reasoning, retention of information, processing information, organisation of information and verbal comprehension.
- WISC-V – Wechsler intelligence scale is a cognitive assessment for children below the age of 16 years.
- BAS 3 – British ability scales can be used to assess children's current intellectual functioning and measures verbal ability, non-verbal reasoning, spatial ability, general conceptual ability, and a special non-verbal composite.
- WIAT – Wechsler individual achievement test measures reading, comprehension and fluency, written expression, mathematics and total achievement [13].

Adaptations and considerations

Once a diagnosis of a learning difference has been reached there is a range of person-centred adaptations that can be implemented in order to support individuals. There is a debate over the proposition that adaptations and strategies should be accessible to all who require them, not just those with a diagnosis. The debate stems from dyslexia not being an 'all or none' condition; there are no clear cut-off criteria, and it is reliant on interpretation. The presentation of dyslexia varies

Table 8.5 Adaptations and considerations

Adaptations and considerations	How this is beneficial
General SpLD	
✓ Extra time in examinations	Provides longer reading, processing and writing time
✓ Interventions that focus on the area of deficit (reading, writing, maths, spelling, vestibular and proprioception)	Provides targeted support for known problem areas
✓ Dictation software ✓ Word processing ✓ Scribes	With strengths in the area of verbal reasoning, dyslexics are often able to articulate and discuss their thoughts and work, yet have difficulty translating these thoughts onto paper.
✓ Visual adjustments-high colour contrasts	Aimed at making letters and words more distinguishable. Using certain fonts and text size can support visual perception when reading.
Dyslexia	
✓ Multisensory teaching	Combining different learning styles (e.g. Visual, Auditory, Kinaesthetic-Tactile VAKT). For example, verbalising a letter sound and name whilst tracing the letter. The use of repetition and overlearning can be a way of embedding learning so that it becomes automatised and readily recalled when needed.
✓ Breaking down and chunking tasks so that they feel more manageable, using a structured approach of small tasks	Aimed at supporting working memory because the smaller sized tasks are easier to remember and gradually become part of routine and move into long term memory
✓ The learning of skills rather than the learning of facts	Using skill sets and problem-solving knowledge rather than facts to solve a problem
✓ Speech-to-text software, read-aloud software	To enable the learner to hear back what they have written
Dyspraxia	
✓ An occupational therapist can assist support with everyday activities at home and school, such as eating, getting dressed, and holding a pen or pencil to write.	Assisted through providing physical supports such as pencil grips and adaptive cutlery

Adaptations and considerations	How this is beneficial
✓ A physiotherapist can help with motor skills.	Aimed at strengthening muscles
✓ A 'task-based' approach called perceptual motor training. This involves practising a series of different tasks repeatedly to ingrain them into muscle memory, thereby making them automatic.	To support short-term working memory as the tasks are repeated and move into long term memory and muscle memory makes them automatic.
✓ Keeping a calendar, making lists and putting things away in an orderly manner. Labelling their drawers and cupboards	Support with organisational difficulties

Dyscalculia

✓ The use of visual aids ✓ The use of number blocks[6] and Numicom[7]	Allows the numbers to be seen and the quantity more easily understood
✓ Mathematical concepts taught and modelled using concrete materials	As visual and practical learners, this strategy enables mathematical problems to be seen rather than being purely theoretical.
✓ Mathematics taught in a procedural way	To provide different ways of solving a problem

Dysgraphia

✓ Using different paper and pens (i.e. paper with thick or raised lines, different weighted and thickness pens)	To provide sensory feedback and support with the fine and gross motor skills required for writing
✓ Cursive writing rather than writing in print	Reduces distraction by spacing; cursive writing has fewer reversible letters and requires a steady movement and flow, which can be beneficial to individuals who have difficulties with fine motor skill.
✓ Audio recordings	Writing can be a cognitively taxing activity, made more difficult when the information has to be read and then written (such as copying text from paper or a board).

in individuals and can change over time depending on daily life challenges and the environment.

Signposting

- British Dyslexia Association – https://www.bdadyslexia.org.uk/
- Dyspraxia UK – https://dyspraxiauk.com/
- Psychologists who are qualified to conduct diagnostic assessments can be found on the British Psychologist website (BPS > Psychologist search > Directory of Chartered Psychologists)
- behaviourhelp.com/a-z-conditions-disorders/
- Dyslexia – NHS
- Developmental co-ordination disorder (dyspraxia) in children – NHS
- https://www.nationalnumeracy.org.uk/

Anya case examples

Dyslexia

Anya is a 36-year-old woman with a diagnosis of dyslexia. Her parents are from a working-class background. Anya received her diagnosis whilst in further education at college. At school she was always told that she did not pay enough attention; she was easily distracted, and she was placed in the bottom classes.

Anya works as a team leader at a local business. This job suits her as she can use her people and creative skills, and she likes being part of a team. Anya struggles with her written work and makes typos and uses the wrong words; her spelling is poor, as is her sentence structure, which is often jumbled and lacks clarity. Anya has short-term memory issues and will often lose the thread of conversations, and is likely to forget if information provided to her is not written down.

Anya uses AI such as 'Chat GPT' and 'Grammarly' to construct her work or emails to improve her written work. She appears to be a very organised person, for example, she prepares her outfits and her work bag the night before, she keeps a diary, calendar, schedules her day and uses lists and Post-its to keep track of tasks.

Phil case examples

Dyspraxia

Phil is an 11-year-old boy who has diagnoses of dyslexia, dyspraxia and autism, which he received at 10 years old. His family are professionals. Phil enjoys sports such as tennis, football and rugby. He enjoys being creative, drawing and gaming. Phil can become obsessed with his interests and will focus on one aspect or subject for long periods. Phil can articulate an argument and can explain himself in detail verbally.

Phil attends a grammar school and has learning adaptations in place such as using a laptop to type rather than handwriting and using a phone to screenshot homework, and he receives a handout summarising the lesson to remove the need to copy from the board. Phil needs reminders to complete his homework and support to structure his time. Phil often needs support from his family to pick out his clothes and he requires step-by-step instructions to get ready in the morning. Phil often masks his challenges with a nonchalant attitude.

Lotus case examples

Dyscalculia

Lotus is a 10-year-old girl, who has a diagnosis of dyslexia and dyscalculia. She is very diligent and is an eager learner even though she struggles with reading and maths. Lotus has had private tutoring outside of school; this did not improve her academic performance.

After investigation, it became clear that Lotus struggled with phonetics and expressing ideas in words. In mathematics, concepts such as fractions were difficult to articulate; however, Lotus was able to interpret symbols and understand the relationship between concrete objects. The school used this knowledge to teach Lotus concepts such as using diagrams and cutting pieces of paper into different parts to assist with the explaining of fractions. Understanding how Lotus learned made it possible to teach mathematical concepts.

Anya case examples

Dysgraphia

Florence is an 8-year-old girl who is very articulate; she loves learning, crafts, swimming, running and cycling. Florence enjoys school and being with her friends; however, she 'hates writing' as it makes her brain and hands tired. Florence comments that she has all the answers in her head and can talk about them but just cannot write them down, which makes her feel angry, and she often gets frustrated.

Florence's school is beginning to explore adaptations for her such as using a Dictaphone, using a scribe, different pencils and pencil grips, and using speech-to-text software and/or a laptop to help her produce her written work.

Notes

1 Centred on or considered in terms of England or Britian.
2 Phonological processing is the use of the sounds of one's language (i.e., phonemes) to process spoken and written language.
3 AMBDA accreditations explained – British Dyslexia Association.
4 wisc-v-uk-brochure-march-2019.
5 AMBDA accreditations explained – British Dyslexia Association.
6 CBeebies number programme *Numberblocks* – BBC iPlayer.
7 'What Is Numicon & Why Is It Important? Early Years Resources: https://www.earlyyearsresources.co.uk

References

1. American Psychiatric Association. (2022). *Diagnostic and Statistical Manual of Mental Disorders* (5th ed., text rev.). American Psychiatric Association.
2. World Health Organisation. (2022). *International Classification of Diseases* (11th Revision). World Health Organisation.
3. British Dyslexia Association. (2018). *Understanding Neurodiversity: A Guide to Specific Learning Differences*. Retrieved from: https://cdn.bdadyslexia.org.uk/uploads/documents/Dyslexia/A_Guide_to_SpLD_2nd_ed.pdf.
4. Grant, D. (2017). *That's the Way I Think: Dyslexia, Dyspraxia, ADHD and Dyscalculia Explained*. London: David Fulton Books.
5. Rose, J. (2009). *Identifying and Teaching Children and Young People with Dyslexia and Literacy Difficulties. An Independent Report from Sir Jim Rose*

to the Secretary of State for Children, Schools and Families. London: Department for Children, Schools and Families.

6. Kirby, P. (2018). *A Brief History of Dyslexia.* Retrieved from: www.dyslexia history.web.ox.ac.uk/brief-history-dyslexia.

7. Critchley, Macdonald (1970). *The Dyslexic Child.* London: Heinemann.

8. Tizard, J. (1972). *Children with Specific Reading Difficulties: Report of the Advisory Committee Great Britain Advisory Committee on Handicapped Children.* UK: Department of Education and Science and H.M. Stationery Office.

9. Warnock, H. M. (1978). *Report of the Committee of Enquiry into the Education of Handicapped Children and Young People.* Kew, London: H.M. Stationary Office

10. Gubby, S. S. (1975). *The Clumsy Child.* Philadelphia PA: W. B. Saunders.

11. VERCIDA. (n.d.) Dyspraxia and Diversity: Dyspraxia across Society. Retrieved from: https://www.vercida.com/uk/articles/dyspraxia-and-diversi ty-dyspraxia-across-society.

12. Davies, M. G. (2022) The White Spaces of Dyslexic Difference: An Intersectional Analysis. Retrieved from: https://ualresearchonline.arts.ac.uk/id/ep rint/22436/4/Chapter%207%20The%20White%20Spaces%20of%20Dyslexic% 20Difference%20An%20intersectional%20Analysis.%28Final%20Pre-publica tion%20copy%29.pdf.

13. Davis, R. (2010). *The Gift of Dyslexia.* London: Souvenir Press.

14. Elliot, J. G. & Grigorenko, E. L. (2024). *The Dyslexia Debate.* Revised ed. Cambridge University Press.

9 Sensory Processing Disorder

Ruth Farrar

OCCUPATIONAL THERAPIST

ⓘ Introduction

Sensory processing is a term that is frequently heard and used but can often be misinterpreted and possibly misunderstood. More and more people are receiving a diagnosis of Sensory Processing Disorder (SPD). Clinicians are more regularly expected to understand the condition and to make adaptions to the interventions that they provide, so that they are more accessible to those who experience these challenges. For example, challenges may include individuals struggling with the noise, light, or temperature of clinic spaces, being unable to sit still for a prolonged period or requiring movement to be able to concentrate. These may seem simple but can be vital to correctly 'set the scene' and offer the best and right environment for intervention/therapy to be meaningful, accessible and effective for people with sensory differences.

Common terminology in this field includes **sensory processing, sensory disorders** and **sensory discrimination**; interventions are often referred to as **sensory strategies, Sensory Integration Therapy**, and **Ayres Sensory Integration**. This chapter will unpick these terms to provide clarity for clinicians and to support their navigation of this area.

Sensory processing difficulties are commonly thought of alongside autism, and a significant proportion of the evidence for sensory processing challenges are associated with the neurodivergent population. However, there is more research evolving into other clinical populations which continue into adulthood and thus span the lifetime. Typically, paediatric settings provide a degree of sensory processing exploration, but depending on the provider and the commissioned service this provision is not consistent within the UK. Additionally, 'treatment' or interventions are often not funded through public services. This often means that individuals seek assessment and intervention from within the private sector.

DOI: 10.4324/9781003510659-9

The emerging evidence and clinical landscape are recognising that within mental health settings, including both Child and Adolescent Mental Health Services (CAMHS) and adult services, there are more neurodivergent individuals seeking support for mental health conditions. These individuals are reporting that sensory based interventions are helpful for them and have been missing in previous interventions that they have been provided. Increasingly, individuals are confirming that they experience difficulties with sensory processing and that they have experienced these throughout their life, but these have previously been attributed to other causes.

This chapter is divided into the following sections:

1   Background
2   Heterogeneity within sensory processing disorder
3   Things to look out for
4   Screening assessments
5   Specialist assessment
6   Adaptations and considerations
7   Signpost services
8   Case examples
9   References

Background

Sensory Integration is the unconscious process whereby our senses provide our body with the information that we receive from our environment. This is important for allowing us to understand the situation that we are in and what our bodies need to do to respond. Sensory processing is vital for us as humans. The primary role is within our internal safety system, which helps us to recognise threats in our environment. It is a part of our parasympathetic nervous system and can often be displayed through our fight, flight or freeze response.

Sensory integration (SI) therapy was founded by Jean Ayres, drawing on the original work from L. J. King, who focused her work on adults with psychosis and difficulties in processing vestibular information. Ayres drew on this work and honed her knowledge of neuroscience and occupational therapy. She observed deficits in both learning and behaviour of the children that she was treating. It was from these observations that she hypothesised that these deficits were due to poor processing of sensation in the central nervous system (CNS). Ayres [1] defined sensory integration as 'the neurological process that organises sensation from one's own body and from the environment and makes it possible to use the body effectively within the environment'. Ayres' theory focused on the vestibular, proprioception and tactile systems predominantly, but she recognised the impact from the other sensory systems and the interplay between them. She acknowledged the difficulty that deficits in sensory systems play in executing a person's activities of daily living.

Alongside the theory's recognition of the dysfunction of sensory systems, a core premise is also that effective sensory integration underpins learning [2]. Ayres referred in her theory to sensory integrative dysfunction, but it was Miller et al. [3] who coined the term SPD in their work, 'a proposed nosology', and went on to categorise SPD as an umbrella term to include Sensory Modulation Disorder (SMD), similar to how Ayres described Modulation, Sensory Based Motor Disorder (SBMD), divided into dyspraxia and postural disorders and Sensory Discrimination Disorder (SDD), focused on the difficulties in specific sensory systems. These terms are more commonly used when talking about sensory processing from sensory trained clinicians, but they are not recognised in the diagnostic criteria of the DSM-5 or the ICD-11, in their own right.

According to Ayres [4], sensory information flows to the brain like water flowing into a stream. The brain must organise, filter and sort this information so that we can respond to it effectively. For example, if you put your hand out onto a hot plate on top of the cooker the sensation travels up to the brain, the brain recognises this as painful, and you react by pulling away quickly. This process happens instantly, but if there is a problem with any part of this sequence, then this simple sequence can be harmful, and the consequence could result in getting burned.

Our sensory systems start developing *in utero* and are vital to our development as a child. They help us interact with our world and simple childhood activities such as going to the park, throwing and catching a ball, and learning to tie our shoelaces are all reliant on our ability to process and use sensory information effectively. It is when these systems do not develop or are not fully developed as we mature, that we begin to notice difficulties in school, home life, work and within relationships.

Humans have eight sensory systems: Gustatory (Taste), Tactile (Touch), Olfactory (Smell), Auditory (Hearing), Vision (sight), Vestibular (Balance response to gravity), Proprioception (Body awareness/body Schema), and Interoception (sensing our internal signals). With the exception of Interoception, our sensory systems are external and are used to interact with and experience the outside world. These sensory systems have receptors which receive the information, which then travels to the brain via a range of different neurological pathways. These meet at the cerebellum and synapse (transfer information from one neuron to another) where they then travel to the receiving site in the brain, the limbic system. Here information is organised and sorted. A response is then sent back down the pathways to our limbs for us to respond appropriately [5].

Interoception is our internal body sense and gives us cues about what we need. For example, it tells us whether we are hot or cold, hungry or thirsty, or might need to go to the toilet. However, describing these feelings accurately can be difficult for some individuals and it is suggested that if we are unable to recognise our core internal cues in a timely way, then this can begin to negatively affect our outward behaviour [6].

Our three foundation sensory systems are vestibular, proprioception and tactile.

- The **vestibular** system has its receptors in the ear, and information travels along similar pathways to the auditory system taking information to the brain. Its primary function is to monitor the position and movement of the head. It gives us our awareness of balance and equilibrium and helps us to coordinate the movement of our head and eyes and helps us adjust our posture [5]. This function is important for individuals to be able to maintain an upright position, interact with gravity and to isolate their head and trunk movements. When there are challenges in this system, movement, posture and balance are affected.
- The **proprioceptive** system represents the sensations of muscle movement providing us with information on speed, sequencing, timing and force, and supports us with joint positioning. It creates a motor map for our bodies and the external environment so that they can interact effectively. This sense is essential for the development of body schema, for praxis and how we produce adaptive responses [2].
- The **tactile** system has its receptors in the skin and therefore is our largest sensory system. Its responsibility is to detect pain and keep our body and internal organs safe. It helps us to discriminate what we are interacting with externally and distinguish objects in our environment. It helps us develop perception and informs our body positions alongside proprioception [5].
- The **visual** system (sight) is the part of the central nervous system that is required for visual perception. It receives, processes and interprets

visual information to build a representation of the visual environment. The information travels via the optic nerve up to the visual cortex of the brain which relays information to inform us. Without vision, other senses can sometimes be heightened and more sensitive [7].

- The **olfactory** system is responsible for smell. It plays a crucial role in detecting smells, again to keep us safe from unpleasant odours. For example, it is usually our smell sense that is the sense that is triggered first. It enables us to detect if food is rotten/inedible and whether we might choose to or avoid eating something. It supports our feeding, self-defence and social interactions. The sensory pathways to the brain operate in isolation initially, so people can often be triggered by a smell sensation quickly, which may elicit the recall of past memories both positive and negative [7].

- The **gustatory** sense (taste) detects, identifies and categorises different taste sensations, the receptors on our tongue being able to differentiate between, sweet, salty, sour, bitter and savoury flavours. This information is sent to our CNS and stored so that we can recall pleasant and unpleasant tastes [5].

- The **auditory** sense (hearing) uses the auditory nerve to carry sound waves received from the environment via the ear. The messages travel to the brain and are turned into sounds which we can recognise and understand. This sense integrates with other sensory systems and supports us to engage in movement, communication, and can guide behaviour [5].

Ayres' original theory describes two main areas of sensory dysfunction: modulation and praxis. Modulation is one's ability to filter sensations appropriately and to attend to those that are relevant whilst still maintaining the right level of alertness or arousal to complete tasks. When modulation is not sufficient for one's needs, then distraction and the ability to remain on task is affected.

Praxis is the ability to practically complete a task, it requires the ability to recognise the incoming sensory information, organise and sequence it and then create the outward action or an adaptive response [4]. The characteristics of praxis include ideation, sequencing, and execution, to enable the delivery of smooth fluid movements. Dysfunction in praxis can be understood through a sensory lens as either bilateral integration and sequencing (BIS) or somatodyspraxia.[1] When there is a difficulty with one of these components then there is praxic dysfunction, commonly referred to as dyspraxia [2].

SPD is not a specified diagnosis in the DSM-5 diagnostic criteria, rather it is often referred to as part of other diagnoses. For example, in

2013, the DSM-5 was revised to include sensory processing as part of the criteria for autism. Additionally, paediatricians may assess and treat SPD in order to improve an individual's daily life. In such cases a sensory assessment is typically undertaken which focuses on praxis, which in turn enables the consultant to make a conclusive diagnosis.

Heterogeneity within sensory processing disorder

Sensory processing can present in many ways; it can feel and present differently for each person. It can often be challenging for individuals to identify exactly what they are experiencing and how to articulate this effectively. The overlap between our sensory experiences and our emotions can complicate this further and feel confusing for people to understand. This said, typical difficulties identified by individuals can include finding certain tastes and textures of food bothersome and uncomfortable, feeling overwhelmed by smells and being able to smell things that others cannot, experiencing acute reactivity to noise and noticing the smallest sounds that other people are able to filter out and would not notice. These experiences can be painful and distressing for the individual. Additional indicators include individuals having difficulty completing everyday tasks, which could highlight a clear signal that sensory processing challenge could be present. Examples may include difficulty participating in personal care tasks such as bathing, washing hair, brushing teeth and sensitivity to items of clothing or difficulties when going out for meals with family and friends. These are often the triggers for behavioural responses that may be perceived as overreactions by others. It is often these behaviours that are noticed by others prior to the behaviour being understood within the context of sensory processing differences.

Additional difficulties with fine and gross motor tasks, seeking and/or avoiding certain tasks are also an important requisite for potential sensory processing difficulties. Sensory processing challenges can change over time and be affected by the environment. Factors such as having a mental health diagnosis, and/or experiencing trauma or having physical disability can also heighten sensory responses to stimuli in the environment.

Below is a consideration of how sensory processing may differ, illustrated through age, gender and in the context of trauma; albeit it should be noted that sensory processing differences are not restricted to these areas.

Age

Our senses develop from birth and our experiences and environments are crucial for our senses to develop and grow appropriately. Our senses are the foundation of our CNS [5] and are the cornerstone of brain development. The brain develops throughout our lifespan, and we can acquire new skills and learning largely due to neuroplasticity, which allows the brain to develop and grow. The greatest period of growth is during childhood and there are consequent significant changes to our sensory development at key stages such as during adolescence.

One of the primary activities to aid development during childhood is 'play', as this affords opportunities to the brain that provide the 'nutrients' it requires to make the connections and expansion it needs to grow. If these opportunities are not available during development, then it is likely that areas of our brain will develop at different times, (either faster or slower) and this can create 'pockets' of underdevelopment that can continue through to adulthood. Challenges can manifest themselves in poor motor coordination, resulting in challenges in gross and fine motor skills which can in turn affect learning. These could include, for example, not being able to hold a pen, inability to use cutlery, having a weak grip for handwriting, or struggling to sit still or upright owing to challenges in postural control. Difficulties with physical activities such as not being able to run, jump or catch a ball may also ensue. Deficits in these areas can begin to affect self-esteem, confidence and self-belief which can remain with individuals throughout their life, affecting relationships, friendships, the ability to work, leisure activities, and may potentially contribute to increased anxiety, depression and feelings of low self-worth. As people transition into adulthood, if sensory challenges have not been identified and addressed, they may potentially be overshadowed by a mental health diagnosis, and individuals may find themselves accessing mental health services for support.

Gender

The term gender refers to the characteristics of men, women, girls and boys that are socially constructed, including norms, behaviours, and roles associated with being a man, woman, girl or boy. Women and girls tend to be good at 'masking' certain behaviours or sensory processing difficulties that they experience. Often, people with sensory processing differences will observe what is considered 'normal' and attempt to mirror this in order to feel included. Women and girls tend to be more governed by the desire to connect with others and to form relationships. Indeed research confirms that females with a diagnosis of autism may wish to engage in sensory soothing behaviours to help them to manage a given situation but are conscious that it would not be socially acceptable to engage in the behaviours/techniques that usually offer them regulation and comfort. As such, females are more likely to wait until they are in a safe place to engage in the behaviours that they find self-soothing. Men and boys are often less socially motivated and so may be more driven by what they need to do/or wish to avoid.

Trauma

People who have experienced trauma are likely to have heightened sensory experiences and can present as hyperalert or hypervigilant to their environment. Alternatively, they may display what could be perceived as indifference to a situation, where in fact they are very much aware of their environment but have developed 'safety behaviours' (i.e. shutting off from external experiences) to cope with the situation and to manage any perceived potential threats. Often people who have experienced trauma retain these experiences through their sensory systems, and sensory stimulation may trigger and remind people of their previous trauma experiences. This client group may report feeling overwhelmed by environments and sensory feedback and have difficulty recognising exactly what they are experiencing, such as having difficulty differentiating between their thoughts, emotions and behaviours.

Mental health

The evidence suggests that people with a mental health condition may also struggle to process sensory information effectively. For example, someone with depression or anxiety may often report feeling lethargic and tired and they may have reduced motivation to complete tasks. Additionally, psychotropic medication may have a dampening effect on their sensory experiences. Therefore, sensory approaches can be invaluable to support individuals in accessing their internal 'wake up systems' to support them to engage more effectively in their occupational activities. For somebody with a diagnosis of bipolar affective disorder or a personality disorder, challenges in feeling regulated and stable can be difficult. For this client group, accessing calming sensory strategies and weaving them into their daily routine can be of benefit.

In summary, this section has offered some considerations for professionals in terms of different client groups and their sensory presentations. It has briefly outlined some of the identifiable traits suggestive of sensory processing difference. Sensory processing rarely is, but can be, standalone in its presentation and more commonly it will accompany a formal diagnosis of a recognised condition. It is important to recognise that everyone experiences sensory information differently, therefore, whilst an individual may present as over alert or exhibit sensory seeking behaviour, these behaviours may be helpful and provide a calming and regulatory function for the individual. A professional trained in sensory difference is thus required to best understand and interpret these subtleties.

Things to look out for

Occupational Therapists are generally well placed to notice the indicators for sensory processing difficulties. They are dual trained[2] and will look predominately at the function of an individual's behaviour. This section will highlight areas for clinicians to consider when working with individuals in different clinical settings across the lifespan. It is a comprehensive but not exhaustive illustration of sensory processing differences and the potential impact that they may have upon an individual's function. Should such differences be identified, a referral to occupational therapy for further sensory exploration may then be relevant. Sensory processing differences often present in distress and/or impairment for the individual; key markers at different phases of the lifespan might include:

- **Preschool:** The child may not meet their developmental milestones. Difficulties could present as an inability to tolerate loud environments such as during play groups or sing-along time. The child might struggle with posture and core control, so the basic tasks of sitting up or sitting still for periods of time that are age appropriate may be difficult. 'Meltdowns' could be an indicator of sensory processing differences and may reflect the child communicating that they are not coping in the given environment, and their behaviour may serve the function of seeking additional feedback to feel calmer. The child may take longer than others to return to their emotional baseline.
- **Children** may engage in sensory seeking or avoiding behaviours and thus choose not to wear certain fabrics, such as finding wearing their school uniform difficult and removing this as soon as they get

home, for example. They may have difficulty with tasks such as tying their shoelaces and getting dressed without support from an adult and/or verbal prompts. They may struggle to integrate into reception or early years school provision, perhaps finding the environment and the number of children that they must share their space with overwhelming. This may lead to 'rough' play or the child being especially active or withdrawn. They may continue to find the lunchtime experience, including the physical environment, distressing because of the noise, smells and volume of people present. They may find gross motor tasks challenging and struggle to catch a ball, kick a ball, ride a bike or learn to swim.

Adolescents may display all of the above indicators as well as experiencing difficulties with the transition to secondary school, which can sometimes be complex and traumatic for individuals with sensory processing difficulties. The additional pressures of navigating and learning a new environment can cause significant overwhelm, and sometimes cause a young person to disengage from school completely. Alternatively, at this stage of development it is common for children who have been very active in sports, clubs and activities such as singing or swimming to withdraw to focus on their studies; they may then experience difficulties because they do not have the physical activities supporting their brain–body engagement, which may have previously allowed them to tolerate their environment. In the absence of this sensory feedback, increases in less adaptive behaviour can sometimes occur.

Adults may have gone through their life on the outskirts of social groups, for example not being picked for sports teams at school owing to their difficulties in motor co-ordination. They might have found socialising awkward due to the social environment being too loud, too bright or too crowded, and they may have struggled to maintain employment. They may experience difficulties to such a degree that this has led them to explore their functional abilities and the impact of their sensory processing, or they may have become aware of their differences via a professional, for example receiving a diagnosis of autism/Attention Deficit Hyperactivity Disorder (ADHD). Adults with a mental health diagnosis often report having always experienced underlying challenges with sensory processing but not previously having attributed these as such.

For older adults, depending on the circumstance, if there has not been an injury or change to their brain function through illness, sensory processing is likely to display itself through over- or under-responding to sensory information (modulation). For example, for a previously active individual who has become physically inactive, this can indicate dysregulation, or an individual becoming under- or over-stimulated could be a clear indicator that they are experiencing sensory processing challenges.

What is clear is that sensory processing can be traced back to childhood/ infancy. The research and theory from Ayres inform us that sensory processing is a developmental process. It is helpful for clinicians to be mindful of how an individual's sensory journey begins right from birth, to appreciate the potential barriers in development of the sensory systems and the impact this can have on function. This said, there are some individuals that may, as an adult or older adult, develop changes in their sensory processing following a physical or psychological trauma or injury.

Screening assessments

If some of the characteristics as described in the previous section have been observed, it is possible that they would benefit from an occupational therapy assessment and a sensory processing assessment. Occupational Therapists are well placed to complete sensory assessments if they have received the specialist training to do so. This is because a core premise of occupational therapy is assessing how a person interacts with their environment and the challenges that they may be experiencing that inhibit their occupational performance. The assessment is always completed through a holistic lens. Other allied health professionals such as Physiotherapists and Speech and Language Therapists who are appropriately trained in Ayres Sensory Integration could also complete the assessments.

It is most likely that an Occupational Therapist would complete the screening assessments for sensory processing difficulties, and then if further, more specialised assessments and intervention were deemed appropriate, a Sensory Integration Practitioner would need to be sought to complete an Ayres Sensory Integration Assessment (trademarked as ASI-r). There are other sensory assessment and interventions such as Sensory Attachment Intervention (SAI) or sensory based intervention (SBI), although these follow a different process. Both ASI and SAI require additional postgraduate training and afford the therapist the skill to hypothesise, and recommend/provide interventions based on the assessment findings. Both these interventions follow clear fidelity measures. Sensory based interventions are normally conducted by therapists who have a level of sensory integration training and/or use sensory informed approaches in their practice but who are not conducting formalised therapy.

For an Ayres Sensory Integration Assessment, consent for the assessment must be gained and background information gathered. It is useful to see if any other clinicians have been or are involved to avoid the individual having to repeat information.

Once initial information is gathered, a developmental history must be obtained, and this is used to understand current strengths and challenges with the individual's functioning. Questions asked may include 'Does the individual have medical diagnosis?' such as anxiety or OCD (as the presence of sensory processing is more apparent with certain diagnoses, for example autism or following a traumatic experience). 'What are the individual's strengths – what are they good at?' 'What do they find difficult?' 'Have these difficulties been present throughout their life or only emerged following a specific event(s)?' 'What was school like for them?' 'Do they work and if so, in what capacity?' 'What are their leisure interests?' These are valuable questions to ascertain a person's current functioning and how any challenges may impact their daily life.

Based on the aforementioned information, a standardised sensory assessment would be considered to gain a more in-depth analysis of the challenges and to enable a working hypothesis to be developed. These assessments could include.

- **Child Sensory Profile** [8] is a parent's questionnaire designed for parents to notice and rate behaviours they have observed in their children. It covers all of the sensory systems and whether the child is experiencing too much or too little feedback, linking this to specific sensory systems.
- **Adolescent/Adult Sensory Profile** [9] gives voice to the individual to determine how the participant processes sensory information in everyday situations. The Sensory Profile involves a questionnaire format that assesses the frequency of responses to certain sensory processing and modulation events as described in the 60 items. This assessment can identify challenges for people and how they may find these forms of sensory processing confusing, upsetting and not meaningful. These can have a particular effect on self-regulation, arousal levels and their ability to modulate their emotions.
- **Sensory Processing Measure (SPM-P, SPM and SPM-2)** is anchored in sensory integration theory [1, 4, 10]. The theory proposes that the processing and integration of sensory inputs is a critical and

neurobehavioural process that strongly affects development. The SPM is an integrated system of rating scales that enables assessment of sensory processing issues, praxis and social participation in pre-school, school age children, adolescent and young adults, adults and older adults. The age of the individual determines whether the SPM-P, SPM or the SPM-2 is used. For all the SPM assessments there is a self-report form and an informant report form (that is completed by parent or carer or partner, or teachers from school/college). The results from the different forms can be compared.

- **Sensory Inventory Revised** is appropriate for all ages. The Sensory Integration Inventory Revised is for individuals with Developmental Disabilities. It is a preliminary assessment for Occupational Therapists who work with people with developmental delays and disabilities. It is designed to screen for clients who might benefit from a sensory integration treatment approach. This tool provides information on the subject's sensory processing abilities and specific self-stimulating or self-injurious behaviours focusing on the tactile, proprioceptive and vestibular systems.
- **Adult/Adolescent Sensory History (ASH) [11]** is designed as a self-report assessment of sensory and motor behaviours commonly observed in individuals with difficulties processing and integrating sensory information. The purpose of this assessment is to help identify adults and adolescents aged 13–95 who experience problems in sensory processing and integration. This measure is designed to identify difficulties in six key areas of functioning: Sensory Systems; Sensory Discrimination; Sensory Modulation; Over-responsivity; Praxis – Motor Coordination and Social-Emotional Functioning.

A clinician with additional sensory training is required to interpret the results of these assessments, and it is best practice to complete these alongside other occupational therapy assessments or models of practice to provide richer information that affords the generation of a clear hypothesis.

A functional assessment of performance is also recommended, along with an additional standardised assessment from a model of practice such as the Model of Human Occupation (MOHO) [12], the Person Environment Occupation, (PEO model) [13], or the Canadian Model of Occupational Performance (CMOP) [14]. These provide the clinician with an overarching understanding of the strengths, challenges and deficits for the individual.

The Royal College of Occupational Therapists (RCOT) confirms that Ayres' sensory integration and sensory based interventions are modalities/ interventions used effectively by Occupational Therapists incorporated into their practice. However, sensory processing challenges should not be viewed in isolation but should be understood as part of an individual's challenges in occupational performance, participation and potential identity, underpinned by broader evidence base and the models of practice mentioned above.

Specialist assessment

A full sensory assessment is often completed by an Occupational Therapist working in the NHS or more likely in private practice. This would be following the Ayres sensory assessment process adhering to the fidelity measure for assessment and intervention [15]. This would include the assessments mentioned previously in the screening assessments sections alongside the developmental history. In addition, some, or all the assessments mentioned below would be completed. These additional assessments offer more comprehensive exploration of an individual's sensory processing, including both modulation and praxis.

- **Sensory Integration & Praxis Test (SIPT)** developed by Ayres [10]: The SIPT has 17 subtests testing various aspects of sensory perception, discrimination, reactivity and contribution to our praxis and ability to participate in everyday life. This is considered the gold standard of sensory processing assessments. This assessment has been around for over 30 years, therefore the EASI is the assessment that will be the next generation of assessment, offering a broader level of standardisation applicable internationally.
- **Evaluation of Ayres Sensory Integration (EASI)** provides a reliable set of tests that assess key sensory integration functions; it measures perception, ocular/postural, bilateral motor coordination, praxis and sensory reactivity. *NB*: this assessment is available in parts but is still undergoing some normative tests and will then be accessible. This test will replace the gold standard SIPT assessment.
- **The Movement Assessment Battery for Children, Third Edition (Movement ABC-3)** provides an objective measurement of gross and fine motor coordination difficulties in children and young adults aged 3–25 years and 11 months.
- **Clinical Observations of Sensory Integration:** Developed by Erna Blanche [16], these are designed for children aged 5–8 years old.

They constitute a set of clinical observations and tasks for an individual to complete in order to gain an insight into a person's level of processing. Often these are used in addition to the other assessments, but can be used where other standardised assessments would not be suitable owing to engagement issues. Subsequently, they have been revised as The Comprehensive Observations of Proprioception – Revised (COP-R) and the Structured Observations of Sensory Integration – Motor (SOSI-M) for age range 5–14 years.

- **Bruininks-Oseretsky Test of Motor Proficiency, 2nd ed., (BOT-2)** [17] will assess fine and gross motor proficiency and focus on stability, mobility, strength, coordination, and object manipulation. This is designed for individuals aged between 4 and 21 years old.

Best practice involves completing a combination of assessments and triangulating the results to ensure a robust comprehensive assessment. Following this, the development of a hypothesis should be offered followed by appropriate intervention. If intervention is required for praxis, this should adopt a bottom-up approach that focuses on the foundation sensory systems first. Intervention should be goal-orientated and follow the fidelity measure to ensure adherence to the treatment modality and have pre- and post-outcome measures. Without this, then intervention is considered to fall under the umbrella of sensory based intervention (SIB).

Adaptations and considerations

The screening assessment will provide a sound level of insight into someone's challenges. It is important to share this information with the individual, being mindful of how they experience sensory information. The following considerations maybe useful to bear in mind when working with individuals who have difficulty processing sensory information.

✓ Offer clear information in a way that is most accessible to them (e.g. email, virtually, face to face, using visual aids, etc.).
✓ Be mindful of additional stimuli during the session (e.g. are you in a room with an extraction fan? Are there lots of distractions from people walking by the window? etc.).
✓ Moderate your tone and volume of voice.
✓ Offer movement breaks to support the brain–body connection to increase their ability to remain focused in the session with you.

✓ Check that the results of your assessments feel relevant to the individual and they reflect the clinical presentation you have observed.

✓ Provide information and psychoeducation to the individual about sensory processing and the sensory systems.

✓ Inform them of relevant groups and support networks (see Signpost section below).

✓ Agree on simple adjustments such as the time and location of your session.

✓ If relevant, complete a sensory ladder with support from the Occupational Therapist to use in your sessions. A sensory ladder is a tool designed to capture any over- and under-responsivity that the individual experiences. It aims to support regulation and uses sensory strategies to support individuals to cope with unwanted overwhelm or the need to seek sensory stimulation. It is client led and individualised.

✓ Be flexible in your approach and utilise strategies to support the individual to engage, such as the use of fidget tools, and or using ear defenders in the waiting room.

✓ Think about your intervention – would a period of sensory interventions be beneficial before engaging in talking therapy (if this is recommended) to allow individuals to access the learning parts of the brain once they have regulation techniques in place?

Signpost services

Learning about sensory processing can often feel like a 'lightbulb' moment for individuals when they come to understand that the challenges that they have been experiencing have a foundation. However, with children, the caregivers often require information to support the child to co-regulate and to enable them to implement the strategies and support weaving them into their daily life. Adults may require support and strategies to develop and understand how they experience sensory challenges and how these impact on their daily life. They may have to implement adaptations to support their engagement in their environment independently.

Below are some resources to support children and adults who experience sensory difficulties and for those supporting them. These websites offer information for parents/carers, individuals and professionals on what sensory processing is, and offer information resources and courses for people wishing to explore and gain a greater understanding of sensory processing.

- https://www.sensoryintegrationeducation.com/
- https://sensoryproject.org/
- https://www.autism.org.uk/ – offers specific information on people with a diagnosis of autism and offers information and support.
- https://www.kelly-mahler.com/ – this website offers information about interoception.

Eli case examples

Eli is an 8-year-old boy with a recent diagnosis of ADHD. He has been prescribed medications for this and although helping, this does not seem to be sufficient to last for a 24-hour period. His parents are reluctant to increase the dose of his medication and hope to try other interventions before reviewing the dose.

Eli has always been an active little boy and was quick to meet his developmental milestones, and once he could walk, he was curious. He would often have bruises from walking into things and falling over. His family report that they must have planned active weekends as Eli is 'on the go' all of the time.

Pre-school and reception went well for Eli but as he moved through to year 1 (5/6 years old) and then year 2 (6/7 years old) he was becoming less confident, enjoying school less and becoming self-critical. At this time his parents requested an occupational therapy assessment to see if there was any additional support to help Eli regulate at home and school and whether any sensory strategies could support Eli.

Following a sensory assessment, it was identified that Eli was having difficulty processing sensory information which was in turn affecting his ability to perform in school. He had difficulty filtering out auditory information and would struggle to know which information was important for him to focus on. He also found it very difficult to sit still and consequently would fidget and become easily distracted. He would lose concentration easily.

A planner was created for Eli for activities at home to support his need for movement to keep him regulated. This also provided his body/brain with the necessary feedback so that he could concentrate for longer. At school he was allowed movement breaks to keep his body active to help his brain to focus, he was given information to keep in front of him, so he did not have to look up to the board or at the teacher, which helped him to minimise environmental distractions and supported his focus. He was allocated a set seat, so that he was familiar with his surroundings so that he was less distracted. He was provided with extra healthy snacks to maintain his energy so that he could sustain his concentration for longer.

Nel case examples

Nel is a 40-year-old female who was referred to adult mental health services; she had been accessing services for several years. Nel had a diagnosis of severe anxiety, and this had begun to impact on her self-esteem. She worked three days a week as an administrative support for a large retail company but had recently been signed off work with work related stress. She was finding it harder to 'do the basics' for herself and her two young children and this was beginning to impact on her family relationships.

Nel was referred via occupational health to occupational therapy to support her with 'activities of daily living' tasks and motivation. She was unsure if this would make a difference as she felt she had engaged with talking therapies in the past and although they offered some level of support, she had been unable to put the taught skills into practice.

Following an OT/SI assessment it was apparent that Nel had spent much of her youth adapting her lifestyle to fit in so that she could function. She reported feeling overwhelmed with basic tasks such as shopping, cooking and laundry. She reported that she hated going to the supermarket and found the experience distressing.

A sensory assessment identified that Nel had trouble processing sensory feedback and that she became easily overwhelmed, which explained some of her current challenges.

Intervention involved adapting Nel's lifestyle to include using online shopping and daily schedules to support her to complete the household jobs and including her family in some of the chores (such as feeding the dog) to share the responsibility of tasks. Sensory calming techniques were used when Nel began to feel overwhelmed which helped her remain in her 'best self' mode (this is referring to when she felt calm and alert enough to complete the tasks she needed to do).

Set times throughout the day were incorporated into Nel's routine, affording her some quiet time so that she had time to process her day and organise her thoughts. This allowed her the space to prioritise tasks that needed to be done or that had arisen during the day, that she had not scheduled for.

Psychoeducation helped Nel to understand what her body needed, and consequently she increased gentle exercise such as yoga to help her feel more balanced and organised. When Nel felt that she was able to return to work, plans to implement these strategies into her working day and alterations to her work environment were applied. Her immediate colleagues were informed (at Nel's request) of techniques that Nel might employ to reduce her sense of overwhelm. She shared what worked with her employer, and this meant that she felt able to return to work and embed the strategies into her work life.

Notes

1 Somatodyspraxia relates to difficulties in coordinating and executing new, rather than habitual, motor tasks. It also involves poor tactile, vestibular and proprioceptive processing.
2 As an Occupational Therapist and Sensory Integration Therapist.

References

1. Ayres, A. J. (1979). *Sensory Integration and the Child.* Los Angeles, CA: Western Psychological Services.
2. Bundy, A.C. & Lane, S.J. (2020). *Sensory Integration Theory & Practice* (3rd Ed.). Philadelphia PA: F.A. Davis Company.
3. Miller, L. J. , Anzalone, M. E., Lane, S. J., Cermak. S. A. & Osten, E. T. (2007). Concept evolution in Sensory Integration: A proposed nosology for diagnosis. *American Journal of Occupational Therapy*, 61(2), 135–142. doi:10.5014/ajot.61.2.135.
4. Ayres, A. J. (2005). *Sensory Integration and the Child*(5th Ed.). Los Angeles, CA: Western Psychological Services.
5. Bear, M. F. & Connors, B. W. (2007). *Neuroscience: Exploring the Brain.* Philadelphia PA: Lippincott Williams and Wilkins.
6. Goodall, E. & Brownlow, C. (2022). *Introception & Regulation.* London: Jessica Kingsley Publishers.
7. Bear, M. F., Connors, B.W. & Paradiso, M. A. (2020). *Neuroscience: Exploring the Brain.* (4th Ed.). Burlington MA: Jones & Barlett Learning.
8. Dunn, W. (2014). *Child Sensory Profile 2.* Pearsons Clinical.
9. Brown, C. E. & Dunn, W. (2002). *Adult/ Adolescent Sensory Profile.* NCS Pearson.
10. Ayres, A. J. (1989). *Sensory Integration and Praxis Test: SIPT Manual* (9th Ed.) Los Angeles, CA: Western Psychological Services.

11. May-Benson, T. (2015). *Adult/Adolescent Sensory History*. OTA. Watertown Primary Care. Cambridge MA: Spiral Foundation. https://thespiralfoundation. org/adult-adolescent-sensory-history-2.
12. Kielhofner, G. (2002). *Model of Human Occupation, Theory and Application*. (3rd Ed.). Philadelphia PA: Lippincott Williams &Wilkins.
13. Law, M., Cooper, B. A., Strong, S., Stewart, D., Rigby, P. & Letts, L. (1996). The Person- Environment-People model: A transactive approach to occupational therapy performance. *Canadian journal of Occupational therapy*, 63. 9–23. doi:10.1177/000841749606300103.
14. Polatajko, H. J., Townsend, E. A. & Craik, J. (2007). Canadian Model of Occupational Performance and Engagement (CMOP-E). In: E. A. Townsend & H. J. Polatajko, *Enabling Occupation II: Advancing an Occupational Therapy Vision of Health, & Justice through Occupation*. P23 Ottawa, ON: CAOT Publications ACE.
15. Schaaf, R. C. & Mailloux, Z. (2015). *Clinicians Guide for Implementing Ayres Sensory Integration*. American Occupational Therapy Association.
16. Blanche, E. I. (2010). *Observations Based on Sensory Integration Theory*. (Clin. Obs.). OT for children. Disc and workbook. Torrance, CA: Paediatric Therapy Network.
17. Bruininks, R. H., Bruininks, B. D. & Bruininks-Oseretsky (2005). *Test of Motor Proficiency: Manual*. Pearson Assessments. Circle Pines, MN: AGS Publishing.

10 Heterogeneity within neurodivergence

Natalie Brotherton

CONSULTANT CLINICAL PSYCHOLOGIST

ℹ️ Introduction

Each chapter of the book thus far has clearly set out information about the reasonable adjustments that might be helpful when working with different specific neurodivergent populations. The current chapter is slightly different in format and aims to provide a discussion around three main areas.

First, heterogeneity within neurodivergent populations will be considered. Second, the issue of differential diagnosis is explored, namely, factors that might be helpful for the clinician to take into account to enhance specificity when differentiating between different neurodivergent profiles, or between characteristics that might be associated with mental health and/or personality-based conditions. Finally, the chapter aims to consider how to approach cases where several neurodivergent profiles co-occur, or they occur alongside diagnosed psychiatric conditions.

This chapter is divided into the following sections:

1 Background
2 Differential diagnosis and neurodivergence
3 Considerations for differential challenges
4 Positive working with neurodivergence
5 Signposting
6 References

🧠 Background

As can be seen from the previous chapters, there can be much overlap of characteristics across different neurodivergent profiles. This does seem somewhat intuitive when we consider an organ as complex as the human brain where a purely modular understanding is inadequate to

DOI: 10.4324/9781003510659-10

reflect the vast neural interconnectivity that exists. Furthermore, there is evidence of shared genetic risk factors between some neurodivergent conditions [1]. Therefore, whilst co-occurring neurodivergence can be expected in some cases, this can present challenges to clinicians, especially where the clinician feels a pressure to 'neatly fit' a person's characteristics into specific categorical diagnostic conceptualisations in order that the individual can gain access to relevant services.

The unique expression of the characteristics of a neurodivergent person is also influenced by their personal and social characteristics (e.g. sexual orientation, gender identity, ethnicity, culture, socio-economic status, language, religious beliefs). For example, autistic and Attention Deficit Hyperactivity Disorder (ADHD) females might express their neurodivergence differently from the stereotypical traits that have often been derived from the observation of males [2, 3].

In addition, neurodevelopmental differences and acquired neurocognitive conditions can co-occur alongside the whole gamut of mental health and personality characteristics. In fact, neurodivergent children and adults experience a higher incidence of co-occurring psychiatric disorders than do their neurotypical peers, and most neurodivergent people experience a co-occurring mental health condition at some point in their life trajectory, and many throughout it [4, 5, 6, 7, 8].

One factor contributing to this relates to neurodivergent people facing more challenges navigating life in a society largely set up to accommodate neurotypical people [9]. As a result, neurodivergent people might 'camouflage' or suppress their neurodivergent characteristics (sometimes unconsciously) and attempt to present a version of themselves that they have learnt might be better accepted by the neurotypical community [10]. For example, a learning-disabled individual might acquiesce due to a lack of understanding, or a fear of outcomes should they express a different opinion to their more able peers; or an autistic person may try to make eye contact with others even though this is extremely uncomfortable for them. Behaving in this way can be mentally exhausting for neurodivergent individuals. Additionally, having to adapt oneself to feel accepted and to 'fit in' can create the belief that one's authentic self is somehow invalid and 'less than', rather than simply being 'different'. People with disability are often ostracised from society and this may intersect with social and personal factors such as gender identification and socioeconomic status, in turn often leading to neurodivergent people being multiply marginalised [11]. Although how risk factors intersect is not entirely clear [12], neurodivergent people, on account of their disability, have an increased risk of experiencing abuse and exploitation [13]. For example, a brain injured person who experiences difficulties with memory and problem solving may fail to understand or process a situation where someone was trying to financially abuse them. Neurodivergent people are also often at a higher risk of exclusion or punishment for behaviour associated with their brain neurology (e.g. a child with unidentified dyslexia or ADHD may be excluded from school because they are experiencing difficulties learning in a neurotypical classroom setting, which has led to them presenting with behavioural challenges). Furthermore, as trauma experiences occur within the context of potential differences in regard to cognitive, attentional, language, sensory, social and emotional understanding and processing for a neurodivergent person, it is hardly surprising that subsequent trauma-related sequelae and mental health symptoms often ensue [14].

For some individuals, their neurodevelopmental traits may be more subtle or 'masked' and, consequently, they may not be identified or assessed until adulthood. Similarly, some individuals who acquire neurocognitive difficulties may not be identified until sometime after the causal event [15]. Consequently, neurodivergent people often live for many years without receiving appropriate support or accommodations. This can mean that they have a chronic experience of having to cope with situations and environments that are unsuitable and sometimes intolerable for them, whilst also lacking access to environments that are fulfilling and that promote their wellbeing.

Differential diagnosis and neurodivergence

An in-depth discussion of diagnosis and differential diagnosis will not be provided here; the reader may wish to refer to the resources in the signposting section below as a starting point. In brief, differential diagnosis comprises a clinical process of differentiating between two or more conditions where the characteristics share commonalities with other neurodevelopmental, neurocognitive, mental health or personality presentations. To date, clear specific biological or genetic markers have not yet been identified to differentiate all neurodivergent presentations, such that the diagnostic decision remains dependent on an individual's qualitative description, direct observation, and ultimately, subjective evaluations by clinicians.

Differential diagnosis associated with neurodivergent conditions has traditionally been the mainstay of paediatricians and psychiatrists. However, it is now accepted that a multi-disciplinary approach for most neurodivergent diagnoses is necessary [16, 17]. Clinicians such as psychologists, speech and language therapists, occupational therapists and nurses are increasingly involved in the process. Operating from this perspective allows each professional to bring their own specialist prism through which they observe the person, such that they may 'spot' things that other clinicians might otherwise overlook (e.g. an occupational therapist 'may' more readily notice sensory difference and a psychologist 'may' be more sensitive to identifying trauma).

Interestingly, particularly within the autistic and ADHD communities, some people are choosing to 'self-identify' or 'self-diagnose' [18, 19]. This seems to be related to factors such as long waiting lists for assessment in public services and the high costs of private assessments, as well as people having increased access to online resourses that possibly enhance individuals' self-awareness. Moreover, for some people it seems that they prefer to trust their own lived experience of neurodivergence rather than undergoing diagnosis from a medical model perspective, which by its nature is 'deficit focused' rather than strength based. Whilst a medical diagnosis is required to access the majority of services, clinicians and services need to adapt to such developments. This may involve making systemic changes in regard to improving diagnostic collaboration with neurodivergent people, and in embracing neuro-affirmative language and processes. There appears to be a move towards developing neuro-affirmative language and practices for working with autistic people [11]; it would be positive to see this approach extended beyond autism and for clinicians to consider how this can be applied to working with all neurodivergent people. It seems equally important, however, that clinicians and services are aware of, and communicate the possible hazards of self-diagnosis such as the increased risk of misdiagnosis and the potential allocation of resources to those with less need at the expense of those with higher levels of impairment or distress [20].

Information gathering

Multiple sources of information should be gathered to assist the differential process. Sources of information that may be helpful dependent on a person's specific case can include:

- Peri- and post-natal information
- Information from previous paediatric examinations
- Genetic testing
- Discussion and/or observation of the child dependent on age and ability

- Discussion with the adult being assessed to find out about their internal experience and their experiences of navigating the world
- Interview with the parent/care giver/teacher of the individual
- Family history and the presence of neurodivergence-genograms can be a clear and concise way of presenting this information
- Rating scales completed by the individual/parent/caregiver/teacher
- Observational data from different environments such as school, home, employment
- Cognitive assessment
- Adaptive functioning assessment
- Neuropsychological assessment
- Assessment of social emotional skills (e.g. those that consider alexithymia, emotion recognition and social cognition)
- Diagnosis-specific validated assessment tools (see previous chapters)
- Vision, hearing, and speech and language assessments
- Sensory assessment
- Literacy skills assessment
- GP/medical records
- School records
- Social services records
- Prison/parole records
- Mental health assessments/diagnostic interview (e.g. SCID; APA)

In many adult cases, particularly those that are referred through social services and/or within a forensic context, there is often the absence of an available caregiver from whom to gain information. In some cases, a family friend, childhood friend or a current friend or partner may be approached with the individual's consent. Whilst this may not provide the same volume or quality of data, some corroborating data are often better than none. However, a neurodivergent individual should not be excluded just because of a lack of informant or developmental information, as this could lead to individuals with support needs failing to have these met. A pragmatic approach may need to be taken in such cases. A multi-disciplinary approach can increase diagnostic confidence in these circumstances.

Considering the 'point' in the person's life trajectory when their differences or difficulties became apparent to them is important, as can ascertaining what was happening within their world at that time. Transitions, changes in relationships, education or employment and physical health problems can be impactful. Cultural factors such as the individual's first language and culturally normative behaviour should be considered (e.g. understanding that diverted eye gaze might reflect social normality in some cultures rather than necessarily being neuro-developmental in nature) [2]. Assessing clinicians should have an awareness of their own cognitive biases and training and consider how these may impact the diagnostic process due to them being more attuned to identifying specific diagnostic presentations.

Irrespective of the 'content' of the information gathered during the assessment, the 'tone' of the process should as far as is possible be collaborative and inclusive. Being asked to reveal personal information or describe behaviour that has potentially been distressing or felt shameful for the neurodivergent person or for their families can be traumatic and, if not handled sensitively, can feel exposing. Being compassionate, curious, and understanding that the person may have faced significant challenges in navigating a neurotypical world may help to validate their experiences.

Considerations for differential challenges

Below is a consideration of some of the common presenting characteristics clinicians might encounter when attempting to differentiate between neurodivergent profiles or between neurodivergence and mental health experiences/personality traits.

It is beyond the scope of this chapter to be exhaustive in respect of all such challenges and the factors set out below, in isolation, cannot differentiate between different presentations. Rather, the following section is intended to raise awareness of some of the diagnoses that share areas of overlap or similarity in presenting characteristics. It aims to prompt a starting point for the clinician's own area of enquiry during the differential process rather than being directive or providing an end point.

Autism and ADHD frequently co-occur. ADHD is reported to be more common in autistic people than vice versa [22]. Whilst the diagnostic criteria do not overlap for the most part, there are some characteristics and behaviours that might be relevant to each group. These include **emotional dysregulation, attentional and executive functioning differences**, and **social differences**; however, the nature of these may differ across conditions.

Social differences for autistic people are often associated with difficulties understanding social intentions and norms. For people with ADHD, social differences often reflect difficulties inhibiting their enthusiastic reward seeking behaviour, which can sometimes override the needs of others and, in turn, lead to peer rejection. Attentional differences for autistic people often reflect their preference to become fully engrossed in an activity of passion or one that has a sensory function; they may pay less attention to the social and emotional behaviour of others. Attentional differences associated with ADHD often pertain to difficulties directing attention flexibly; instead they may fail to sustain attention in some contexts when needed and intensely focus attention on others.

Autistic people may experience emotional 'meltdowns' in response to change or sensory overwhelm. For people with ADHD, emotional outbursts more likely reflect emotional instability, poor self-control or impulsivity. Increased body movements can be associated with autism and ADHD; for the former these will likely be 'stereotypical' or repetitive in nature and for the latter, these are more likely to relate to a sense of 'restlessness' and an urge to be active.

Autism and obsessive-compulsive disorder (OCD): Shared characteristics can include **preference for routines, repetitive behaviour, and compulsive-like behaviour.** One key consideration in their differentiation is that in OCD, obsessions and compulsions are typically distressing for the individual (ego dystonic, that is inconsistent with the person's goals and self-concept). For autistic individuals, intense interests or repetitive behaviour, like stimming, is often soothing and ego syntonic (in harmony with their goals). Repetitive behaviour can occur in people with OCD but it is generally not stereotyped and it is more likely to be anxiety driven and aimed at preventing a perceived negative event from occurring (e.g. 'If I do not engage in a specific behaviour in a specific order, someone I love will get hurt'). For autistic people, repetitive behaviour often facilitates predictability (e.g. lining up toys or completing activities in exactly the same way). However, OCD and autism do co-occur and OCD occurs more frequently in autistic people than within the general population [23, 24].

Autism and anxiety disorders: Anxiety for autistic people is often experienced in the context of change, sensory overload, or social situations because they are experienced as unpredictable and difficult to navigate. Anxiety commonly co-occurs in autism [25].

Autism, attachment and trauma responses: Identifying whether a person's behaviour is associated with autism or due to an impoverished childhood environment, lack of a secure attachment or a subsequent traumatic experience is a frequent dilemma. Of course, there are some people for whom all of these experiences are relevant; however, there are several key differentiating factors. **The Coventry Grid** [26] is an instrument that can be helpful in differentiating between attachment difficulties and autism in children, and compares how each group might express characteristics across several domains. An adult version of the Coventry Grid compares autism and **complex trauma** [27].

Observable differences in **language, cognition, and emotional, social and sensory functioning** are often apparent in autistic people and those with poor attachments or experiences of trauma. A key point is the different 'flavour' of each profile [28], a strong cognitive approach to the world being more typical in autism and a strong emotional approach more common for attachment/trauma (being hypervigilant and sensitive to the emotions of others). Sitting outside of social groups is often common to each profile; autistic people may experience difficulties understanding social expectations and have a sense that they do not 'fit in', whereas people who have experienced significant trauma may find groups difficult because they feel that others are unsafe.

Information may be processed differently by each group; autistic people might have a tendency to notice details and have problems filtering relevant information. People who have experienced trauma might be drawn to information that is more emotionally charged (e.g. whether someone is talking in a threatening way) and they may be unable to divert their attention once noticed. Trauma may lead to intrusive memories or flashbacks, which are not associated with autism.

Onset is another important distinguisher (e.g. did the characteristics emerge following a traumatic experience?). Repetitive play in people who have experienced trauma may reflect trauma processing, re-enactment and emotional regulation, whereas for autistic children, repetitive play may serve a sensory function and be associated with maintaining routine and predictability in their environment.

Autism and schizoid personality disorder: Proneness to isolation and **limited emotional expression** may be present in both groups and can sometimes lead to these presentations being confused. For people with a schizoid profile there appears to be a **lack of social motivation** or interest, whereas autistic people may find relationships difficult because they experience **differences in their social communication and interaction skills**. Autistic people may experience pleasure in intense passions but may not demonstrate their emotions through facial expression or gesture, whereas a person with a schizoid personality style may experience flattened affect and gain little pleasure from activity.

Autism and anxious avoidant personality disorder: People who have an avoidant presentation avoid interpersonal contact due to a **fear of criticism, disapproval or rejection**; they view themselves as inept, personally unappealing, or inferior and inadequate around others. For autistic people, social contact is often avoided because of **social communication difficulties, confusion about social expectations and limited social interaction skills.** Negative experiences with others may impact their willingness to engage socially. People who have autism show repetitive behaviours and interests, whilst individuals with avoidant personality style generally do not show a fixation toward repetitive behaviour.

Autism and Borderline Personality Disorder/Emotionally Unstable Personality Disorder/Complex-Post Traumatic-Stress-Disorder share commonalities [29]. Some individuals have been misdiagnosed with BPD/EUPD [30] when in fact they are autistic, and they may endure negative experiences as a result [31]. This seems to be particularly prevalent in females associated with observed differences in **interpersonal and affective functioning, self-identity and the presence of self-injurious behaviour.** Understanding the function of behaviour can be helpful in considering these factors.

For an autistic person, self-injury may serve a sensory function or be used to manage sensory, social or emotional overwhelm, whereas in BPD/EUPD this is often an expression of the person's intense emotional suffering associated with severe and chronic abuse experiences.

For autistic people, difficulties with self-identity may be associated with differences in understanding abstract concepts such as the self. Masking may also be mistakenly assessed as confused identify. This is in contrast to the unstable identity usually associated with BPD/EUPD that is related to an instability of thoughts, feelings and behaviour.

Emotional dysregulation for autistic people is often associated with differences in recognising and identifying their emotional states and therefore being unable to apply strategies that could help them to regulate. Dysregulation in BPD/EUPD is typically associated with an extreme and fluctuant reactivity of mood.

It should be noted that a **personality disorder diagnosis/misdiagnosis, particularly BPD/EUPD can be highly stigmatising [30]** and impactful on the treatment that the individual receives from others including professionals. This should therefore be managed with **great empathy, care and respect**. A formulation approach that validates the reported and observed characteristics as understandable coping responses to trauma is essential.

Autism spectrum disorder and psychopathy: Although psychopathy is not a formal diagnosis, it is included here because this clinical profile has often been misidentified in autistic people, primarily associated with both presentations being perceived as comprising a **'lack of empathy'**. Understanding the nature of any differences with empathic functioning is key.

In adults, psychopathic traits are suggested to be associated with diminished **affective empathy** whilst retaining **cognitive empathy**. Essentially, psychopathic individuals do not typically 'experience' emotion, but they usually understand that others do and, in some instances, they may use this knowledge for their own self-interest.

For autistic people, the opposite is typically the case, having intact affective empathy and poorer cognitive empathy. That is, autistic people often experience alexithymia (identifying, understanding and describing their feelings) as well as activities requiring Theory of Mind (the ability to attribute mental states such as beliefs, intents, desires, emotions, and knowledge to another or oneself). However, autistic people do 'feel' emotions and for some, their emotions are experienced extremely intensely.

Learning disability (LD) and autism: LD can impact many aspects of an individual's functioning, the diagnosis itself being based on 'global' rather than specific difficulties. A key distinguisher can be identified through examining repetitive and restricted behaviours, as these are not typically present in those with LD.

ADHD and substance use disorders can be difficult to differentiate and often co-occur. Gaining a clear **developmental history** and **age of onset** of ADHD characteristics can be one distinguishing factor. Obtaining detailed information about the person's history of substance misuse and the type of substances that they typically use can inform the differential formulation (although not diagnostic in and of itself). For example, neurodivergent people often (but not always nor exclusively) use substances to manage their characteristics associated with their neurotype (e.g. a person with ADHD may use stimulant-based substances to assist with focus or cannabis to aid sleep). An individual who is managing symptoms resulting from trauma may use opiate-based substances or alcohol to 'numb' themselves, thus providing relief from distressing memories.

ADHD and Foetal Alcohol Syndrome (FAS): The presentation of these conditions can be remarkably similar and can include differences with **executive function, planning, processing speed, memory, and attention** [32].

An obvious distinguisher is a known history of in-utero alcohol exposure. People with FAS often have specific facial features (they may have an upturned nose, smooth philtrum, thin upper lip and epicanthal folds) thus, this can be a helpful distinguisher. Sometimes people with FAS may also be of smaller stature and have a small head size (microcephaly). These features are not associated with ADHD.

ADHD and bipolar disorder: Emotional dysregulation, inattention and impulsivity in both groups can lead to diagnostic uncertainty. However, individuals who experience bipolar symptoms may be grandiose, have fleeting thoughts and ideas, experience periods of extreme mood states, being elevated (mania) or agitated followed by periods of depression.

Emotional dysregulation in ADHD has a different quality, being chronic rather than episodic in nature. The shifting of **attention** and ideas is often more lucid in ADHD than that experienced in bipolar disorder. The manic behaviour in bipolar disorder is often goal directed rather than the **restlessness hyperactivity** seen in ADHD.

Finally, ADHD is neurodevelopmental, therefore onset will be in childhood whereas the onset for people who experience bipolar features is typically late adolescence to early adulthood [33].

ADHD and conduct disorder: Both groups may engage in behaviour that can be **disruptive and hyperactive,** and they may experience **difficulties controlling their emotions and impulses.** Children and adults with ADHD, however, do not typically violate the rights of others or challenge societal norms

Learning Disability (LD) and specific learning disorders: LD comprises **general learning challenges** often caused by broader factors such as medical conditions and environmental factors. Specific Learning Disorders comprises **diagnosable impairments in well-defined academic areas** that are linked to neurodevelopmental differences affecting brain function.

ADHD and specific learning disorders commonly co-occur but can also have several distinct differences. At its core, ADHD presents difficulties with inattention, hyperactivity and impulsivity as well as with executive function, whereas SLDs typically comprise limitations in specific academic processes. Someone with an SLD may have difficulty acquiring specific skills, whereas in ADHD, organising, focusing, and staying on task can be challenging. Behavioural (e.g. impulsivity) and emotional (i.e. instability) difficulties can sometimes be present for people with ADHD, whereas in SPLDs such presentations are often secondary, associated with frustration.

Differentiating brain injury from other neurodivergence: This is clearly much simpler when an injury is reported. Scans and neuropsychological assessment (see the discussion of ABI in Chapter 4) provide vital information. Although differences in inattention, lack of motivation, and poor problem solving might equally be associated with ADHD, depression, and LD, respectively.

It is important to note that brain injury can and does occur in the context of pre-existing neurodivergence, both diagnosed and undiagnosed. Detailed information gathering in respect of pre-morbid cognitive, executive, social and emotional functioning can therefore enhance the understanding of an individual's unique presentation.

Positive working with neurodivergence

As clinicians typically working within the context of expensive and finite resources, the preference is to first aim for diagnostic specificity, where possible. Whilst taking a broader view can provide a holistic understanding of the individual, this can sometimes be to the detriment of precision. Some of the advantages of having a single diagnosis include:

- Providing a more specific route to relevant psychoeducation and post-diagnostic support
- Clearer guidance on empirically based treatment recommendations and prognosis (such as via NICE guidelines)
- Access to the correct services and provisions such as educational plans (e.g. Education, Health and Care Plan), health plans, support with employment (e.g. reasonable adjustments in line with the Equality Act 2010 and Access to Work) and social care funding (e.g. in line with the Care Act 2014)
- Access to benefits where relevant (e.g. Personal Independence Payment)
- Guidance on what might be reasonable accommodations for the individual (although these are generally personal to the individual rather than to any diagnosis)
- Homogeneity and precision can be helpful for research endeavour in respect of understanding specific conditions

Having multiple diagnoses can impact upon the timely receipt of care, as the various 'diagnosis specific' services may experience uncertainty about which service is best placed to support the person and whether they feel that their staff are suitably trained to provide support or intervention. In such cases an impasse may arise whilst services agree who should take a lead. This can mean that the individuals most in need of support could fail to receive this until the point when they reach crisis [34]. Notwithstanding this, as stated, neurodivergent people often do have co-occurring conditions, and it seems that the incidence of individuals receiving multiple diagnoses is becoming increasingly common [35].

It can be difficult to simplify information when a neurodivergent person has co-occurring diagnoses and distress. The aim is to develop a shared understanding that is meaningful and helpful for the individual, for their loved ones (where relevant) and for other professionals. A formulation approach can assist in this regard.

A formulation is a collaborative process undertaken between the clinician and client, and is a summary of an individual's characteristics and behaviour and how these link to that person's past and current experiences. The framework that clinicians adopt towards formulation is often based on their own training and preferred psychological orientation (e.g. attachment, schema, compassion focused), or it may be led by the framework in place within the service in which they work. Some formulation frameworks that are not as tightly bound to any specific therapeutic model (such as the 'five P's' model) [36] are widely used. Another is the Power Threat Meaning framework [37].

This meta-framework contextualises personal distress as a meaning making response to aversive situations. It is an alternative to more traditional psychiatric models; it rejects pathologising language and reasoning and incorporates an individual's strengths. This can provide an empathic and validating approach for working with neurodivergent people who experience co-occurring distress and who, as has been previously discussed in this chapter, have often been marginalised and disempowered within a neurotypical society. The development and communication of any formulation would require adaptation to meet the neurodivergent person's specific abilities and needs.

Regardless of the framework utilised, formulation can be helpful when a co-occurring behaviour of concern, or distress is present, both to increase the understanding of the origin of distress and to direct therapeutic intervention. This is not always relevant in the context of neurodivergence where reasonable adjustments rather than intervention are often indicated.

It is essential that any information communicated about the neurodivergent person's support needs and required adjustments is accessible. A clear and concise summary profile sheet bringing together their strengths, support needs and the accommodations that should be in place can be helpful. This information should be ethical, respectful, collaborative and adapted to be accessible to the individual. Neuro-affirmative 'identity first' language [11] may be relevant but should ultimately be led by the individual's ascertained preferences. Adaptations may comprise pictorial documentation, literal language, large bold print, or audio recorded information, for example. As there is a high prevalence of neurodivergence within families [38], in cases where information is being communicated more widely, it can be prudent to take universal precautions to improve accessibility for all.

Organising the personal profile sheet into domains such as sensory, social, emotional, cognitive, and executive functioning, along with the person's strengths, needs, required adjustments and interventions, can accommodate multi-diagnostic information. Information pertaining to communication needs can also be incorporated; however, in complex cases and for people with specific communication needs, a communication passport [39] may also be required. Finally, where possible, universal adjustments can be set as standard practice in services and spaces that neurodivergent people access. For example, providing quiet areas, avoiding harsh lighting and providing easy-read and pictorial information. Similarly, given the prevalence of victimisation within neurodivergent populations [40], ensuring that staff and services are 'trauma informed' [41] may assist in better engaging neurodivergent people in environments that feel safe to them.

Signposting

Diagnosis

- American Psychiatric Association. (2013). *Diagnostic and Statistical Manual of Mental Disorders* (5th ed.).
- American Psychiatric Association. (2022). *Diagnostic and Statistical Manual of Mental Disorders* (5th ed., text rev.).
- American Psychiatric Association. (2022). *DSM-5-TR Handbook of Differential Diagnosis.*
- Royal College of Psychiatry website: https://www.rcpsych.ac.uk.
- World Health Organization. (2022). *ICD-11: International Classification of Diseases* (11th revision). https://icd.who.int/.

Coventry grid

- Moran, H (2010). Clinical observations of the differences between children on the autistic spectrum and those with attachment problems: the Coventry Grid: *Good Autism Practice*, 11(*2*), 46–59.
- Cox, C., Bulluss, E., Chapman, F., Cookson, A., Flood, A. & Sharp, A. (2019). The Coventry Grid for adults: A tool to guide clinicians in differentiating complex trauma and autism. *Good Autism Practice*, 20(*1*).

Formulation

- The Power Threat Meaning Framework. Find at: https://cms.bps.org.uk/sites/default/files/2022-07/PTM%20Framework%20%28January%202018%29_0.pdf.
- Johnstone, L. & Boyle, M. with Cromby, J., Dillon, J., Harper, D., Kinderman, P., Longden, E., Pilgrim, D. & Read, J. (2018). *The Power Threat Meaning Framework: Overview.* Leicester: British Psychological Society.

References

1. Ronald, A., Simonoff, E., Kuntsi, J., Asherson, P. & Plomin, R. (2008). Evidence for overlapping genetic influences on autistic and ADHD behaviours in a community twin sample. *Journal of Child Psychology and Psychiatry.* 49(5), 535–542. doi:10.1111/j.1469-7610.2007.01857.x.
2. Lai, M. C., Lombardo, M. V., Auyeung, B., Chakrabarti, B. & Baron-Cohen, S. (2015). Sex/gender differences and autism: Setting the scene for

future research. *Journal of the American Academy of Child and Adolescent Psychiatry*, 54(1), 11–24. doi:10.1016/j.jaac.2014.10.003.

3. Young, S., Adamo, N., Ásgeirsdóttir, B. B., Branney, P., Beckett, M., Colley, W., Cubbin, S., Deeley, Q., Farrag, E., Gudjonsson, G., Hill, P., Hollingdale, J., Kilic, O., Lloyd, T., Mason, P., Paliokosta, E., Perecherla, S., Sedgwick, J., Skirrow, C., Tierney, K., ... &Woodhouse, E. (2020). Females with ADHD: An expert consensus statement taking a lifespan approach providing guidance for the identification and treatment of attention-deficit/ hyperactivity disorder in girls and women. *BMC Psychiatry*, 20(1), 404. doi:10.1186/s12888-020-02707-9.

4. Lai, M. C., Kassee, C., Besney, R., Bonato, S., Hull, L., Mandy, W. & Ameis, S. H. (2019). Prevalence of co-occurring mental health diagnoses in the autism population: a systematic review and meta-analysis. *The Lancet Psychiatry*, 6(10), 819–829. doi:10.1016/S2215-0366(19)30289-5.

5. Choi, W. S., Woo, Y. S., Wang, S. M., Lim, H. K. & Bahk, W. M. (2022). The prevalence of psychiatric comorbidities in adult ADHD compared with non-ADHD populations: A systematic literature review. *PloS one*, 17(11). doi:10.1371/journal.pone.0277175.

6. Mazza, M. G., Rossetti, A., Crespi, G. & Clerici, M. (2020). Prevalence of co-occurring psychiatric disorders in adults and adolescents with intellectual disability: A systematic review and meta-analysis. *Journal of Applied Research in Intellectual Disabilities: JARID*, 33(2), 126–138. doi:10.1111/jar.12654.

7. Francis, D. A., Caruana, N., Hudson, J. L. & McArthur, G. M. (2019). The association between poor reading and internalising problems: A systematic review and meta-analysis. *Clinical Psychology Review*, 67, 45–60. doi:10.1016/j.cpr.2018.09.002.

8. National Institute for Health and Care Excellence. (2016). Mental health problems in people with learning disabilities: Prevention, assessment and management. Retrieved from: http://www.nice.org.uk.

9. Grove, R., Clapham, H., Moodie, T., Gurrin, S. & Hall, G. (2023). 'Living in a world that's not about us': The impact of everyday life on the health and wellbeing of autistic women and gender diverse people. *Women's Health* (London), 19. doi:10.1177/17455057231189542.

10. Price, D. (2022). *Unmasking Autism: Discovering the New Faces of Neurodiversity*. New York: Harmony Books.

11. Hartman, D., O'Donnell-Killen, T., Doyle, J. K., Kavanagh, D. M., Day, D. A. & Azevedo, D. J. (2023). *The Adult Autism Assessment Handbook: A Neurodiversity Affirmative Approach*. London: Jessica Kingsley Publishers.

12. Lambert, I., Wright, N., Gardner, A., Fyson, R., Abubakar, A. & Clawson, R. (2024). Cognitive Impairment as a vulnerability for exploitation: A scoping review. *Trauma, Violence, & Abuse*, 1. doi:10.1177/15248380241282993.

13. Child Welfare Information Gateway. (2018, January). Risk and prevention of maltreatment of children with disabilities. Retrieved from: http://www.childwelfare.gov.

14. Rumball, F. (2019). A systematic review of the assessment and treatment of posttraumatic stress disorder in individuals with autism spectrum disorders. *Review Journal of Autism and Developmental Disorders*, 6(3), 294–324. doi:10.1007/s40489-40018-0133-0139.
15. Marco, C. A., Snoad, T. B. L., Poisson, C. & Flamm, A. (2023). Delayed diagnosis of intracranial trauma. *Cureus*, 15(10). doi:10.7759/cureus.47738.
16. National Institute for Health and Care Excellence. (2022). Autism spectrum disorder in adults: Diagnosis and management. Retrieved from: www.nice.org.uk/guidance/cg142.
17. National Institute for Health and Care Excellence. (2019). Attention deficit hyperactivity disorder: Diagnosis and management. Retrieved from: https://www.nice.org.uk/guidance/ng87.
18. Overton, G. L., Marsà-Sambola, F., Martin, R.*et al.* (2023). Understanding the self-identification of autism in adults: A scoping review. *Rev J Autism Dev Disord*, 11. doi:10.1007/s40489-40023-00361-x.
19. British Psychological Society. (2023). 'ADHD is presented as a quirky thing … it's almost become entertainment'. *The Psychologist*. Retrieved from: https://www.bps.org.uk/psychologist/adhd-presented-quirky-thing-its-almost-become-entertainment.
20. David, A. S. & Deeley, Q. (2024). Dangers of self-diagnosis in neuropsychiatry. *Psychological Medicine*, 54(6), 1057–1060. doi:10.1017/S0033291724000308.
21. de Leeuw, A., Happé, F. & Hoekstra, R. A. (2020). A conceptual framework for understanding the cultural and contextual factors on autism across the globe. *Autism Research: Official Journal of the International Society for Autism Research*, 13(7), 1029–1050. doi:10.1002/aur.2276.
22. Young, S., Hollingdale, J., Absoud, M., Bolton, P., Branney, P., Colley, W., Craze, E., Dave, M., Deeley, Q., Farrag, E., Gudjonsson, G., Hill, P., Liang, H. L., Murphy, C., Mackintosh, P., Murin, M., O'Regan, F., Ougrin, D., Rios, P., Stover, N., … & Woodhouse, E. (2020b). Guidance for identification and treatment of individuals with attention deficit/hyperactivity disorder and autism spectrum disorder based upon expert consensus . *BMC Medicine* 18(146). doi:10.1186/s12916-020-01585-y.
23. Meier, S. M., Petersen, L., Schendel, D. E., Mattheisen, M., Mortensen, P. B. & Mors, O. (2015). Obsessive-Compulsive Disorder and Autism Spectrum Disorders: Longitudinal and offspring risk. *PloS one*, 10(11), doi:10.1371/journal.pone.0141703.
24. Aymerich, C., Pacho, M., Catalan, A., Yousaf, N., Pérez-Rodríguez, V., Hollocks, M. J., Parellada, M., Krebs, G., Clark, B. & Salazar de Pablo, G. (2024). Prevalence and correlates of the concurrence of Autism Spectrum Disorder and Obsessive-Compulsive Disorder in children and adolescents: A systematic review and meta-analysis. *Brain sciences*, 14(4), 379. doi:10.3390/brainsci14040379.
25. Kent, R. & Simonoff, E. (2017). Prevalence of anxiety in Autism Spectrum Disorders. In: *Anxiety in Children and Adolescents with Autism Spectrum*

Disorder: Evidence-Based Assessment and Treatment (pp. 5–32). Advance online publication. Elsevier.

26. Flackhill, C., James, S., Soppitt, R. & Milton, K. (2017). The Coventry Grid Interview (CGI): Exploring autism and attachment difficulties. *Good Autism Practice (GAP)* 18, 62–80. Retrieved from: file:///C:/Users/hannah.carton2/Downloads/GAP_Spring_2017_article_81Flack-HillJamesSoppitt MiltonGAP2017%20(1).pdf

27. Cox, C., Bulluss, E., Chapman, F., Cookson, A., Flood, A. &Sharp, A. (2019). The Coventry Grid for adults: A tool to guide clinicians in differentiating complex trauma and autism. *Good Autism Practice (GAP)*, 20, 1. Retrieved from: https://samsonandbulluss.com/application/files/1016/4799/7666/Cox_Bulluss_et_al_May_19_GAP.pdf.

28. Moran, H (2010). Clinical observations of the differences between children on the autistic spectrum and those with attachment problems. The Coventry Grid. *Good Autism Practice*, 11(2), 46–59. Retrieved from: https://www.johnwhitwell.co.uk/wp-content/uploads/2014/05/The CoventryGrid_2010.pdf.

29. Sarr, R., Spain, D., Quinton. A. M. G., Happé, F., Brewin, C.R., Radcliffe, J., Jowett, S., Miles, S., González, R.A., Albert, I., Scholwin, A., Stirling, M., Markham, S., Strange, S. & Rumball, F. (2025). Differential diagnosis of autism, attachment disorders, complex post-traumatic stress disorder and emotionally unstable personality disorder: A Delphi study. *British Journal of Psychology*, 116, 1–33. doi:10.1111/bjop.12731.

30. Tamilson, B., Eccles, J. A. & Shaw, S. C. K. (2024). The experiences of autistic adults who were previously diagnosed with borderline or emotionally unstable personality disorder: A phenomenological study. *Autism*, 29 (2). doi:10.1177/13623613241276073.

31. May T., Pilkington P. D., Younan R. &Williams K. (2021). Overlap of autism spectrum disorder and borderline personality disorder: A systematic review and meta-analysis. *Autism Research*, 14 (12), 2688–2710. doi:10.1002/aur.2619.

32. Peadon, E. & Elliott, E. J. (2010). Distinguishing between attention-deficit hyperactivity and foetal alcohol spectrum disorders in children: Clinical guidelines. *Neuropsychiatric Disease and Treatment*, 6, 509–515. doi:10.2147/ndt.s7256.

33. Salvi, V., Ribuoli, E., Servasi, M., Orsolini, L. & Volpe, U. (2021). ADHD and Bipolar Disorder in adulthood: Clinical and treatment implications. *Medicina (Kaunas, Lithuania)*, 57(5), 466. doi:10.3390/medicina57050466.

34. Department of Health. (2021). Policy paper: National strategy for autistic children, young people and adults: 2021 to 2026. Retrieved from: https://www.gov.uk/government/publications/national-strategy-for-autistic-children-young-people-and-adults-2021-to-2026/the-national-strategy-for-autistic-children-young-people-and-adults-2021-to-2026.

35. McGrath, J. J., Lim, C. C. W., Plana-Ripoll, O., Holtz, Y., Agerbo, E., Momen, N. C., Mortensen, P. B., Pedersen, C. B., Abdulmalik, J., Aguilar-Gaxiola, S., Al-Hamzawi, A., Alonso, J., Bromet, E. J., Bruffaerts, R., Bunting, B., de Almeida, J. M. C., de Girolamo, G., De Vries, Y. A., Florescu, S., Gureje, O., … & de Jonge, P. (2020). Comorbidity within mental disorders: A comprehensive analysis based on 145,990 survey respondents from 27 countries. *Epidemiology and Psychiatric Sciences*, 29. doi:10.1017/S2045796020000633.
36. Weerasekera, P. (1996). Formulation: A multiperspective model. *Canadian Journal of Psychiatry*, *38*(5). doi:10.1177/070674379303800513.
37. Johnstone, L. & Boyle, M. with Cromby, J., Dillon, J., Harper, D., Kinderman, P., Longden, E., Pilgrim, D. & Read, J. (2018). *The Power Threat Meaning Framework: Overview*. Leicester: British Psychological Society.
38. Hope, S., Shadrin, A. A., Lin, A., Bahrami, S., Rødevand, L., Frei, O., Hübenette, S. J., Cheng, W., Hindley, G., Nag, H., Ulstein, L., Efrim-Budisteanu, M., O'Connell, K., Dale, A. M., Djurovic, S., Nærland, T. & Andreassen, O. A. (2023). Bidirectional genetic overlap between autism spectrum disorder and cognitive traits. *Translational Psychiatry*, 13(1), 295. doi:10.1038/s41398-023-02563-7.
39. Millar, S. (1991). *CALL Scotland*. Blog. https://www.callscotland.org.uk.
40. Trundle, G., Jones, K. A., Ropar, D. & Egan, V. (2023). Prevalence of victimisation in autistic individuals: A systematic review and meta-analysis. *Trauma, Violence & Abuse*, 24(4), 2282–2296. doi:10.1177/15248380221093689.
41. Department for Health Improvement and Disparities. (2022). Working definition of trauma-informed practice. Retrieved from: https://www.gov.uk/government/publications/working-definition-of-trauma-informed-practice/working-definition-of-trauma-informed-practice.

Index

186   *Index*

For Product Safety Concerns and Information please contact our EU
representative GPSR@taylorandfrancis.com
Taylor & Francis Verlag GmbH, Kaufingerstraße 24, 80331 München, Germany

* 9 7 8 1 0 3 2 8 3 9 7 8 3 *